HOW THE SHAMAN
STOLE THE MOON

Books by William H. Calvin

Inside the Brain:
Mapping the Cortex, Exploring the Neuron
with GEORGE A. OJEMANN
(1980)

The Throwing Madonna:
Essays on the Brain
(1983, 1991)

The River That Flows Uphill:
A Journey from the Big Bang to the Big Brain
(1986)

The Cerebral Symphony:
Seashore Reflections on the Structure of Consciousness
(1989)

The Ascent of Mind:
Ice Age Climates and the Evolution of Intelligence
(1990)

How the Shaman Stole the Moon:
In Search of Ancient Prophet-Scientists
from Stonehenge to the Grand Canyon
(1991)

HOW THE SHAMAN
STOLE THE MOON

IN SEARCH OF ANCIENT
PROPHET-SCIENTISTS
FROM STONEHENGE TO
THE GRAND CANYON

William H. Calvin

WITH ILLUSTRATIONS BY MALCOLM WELLS
AND PHOTOGRAPHS BY THE AUTHOR

BANTAM BOOKS
NEW YORK · TORONTO · LONDON · SYDNEY · AUCKLAND

HOW THE SHAMAN STOLE THE MOON
A Bantam Book / December 1991

ACKNOWLEDGMENTS

Portions of this book have been adapted from an article
by the author that appeared in the *Whole Earth Review*
(Spring 1991).

BOOK DESIGN BY GRETCHEN ACHILLES

Library of Congress Cataloging-in-Publication Data

Calvin, William H., 1939–
How the Shaman stole the moon : in search of ancient prophet-
scientists : from Stonehenge to the Grand Canyon / William H.
Calvin.
p.   cm.
Includes bibliographical references and index.
ISBN 0-553-07740-6
1. Astronomy, Prehistoric.   2. Eclipses.   I. Title.
GN799.A8C35   1991
520'.93—dc20   91-13528
                                                       CIP

Published simultaneously in the United States and Canada

Bantam Books are published by Bantam Books, a division of Bantam
Doubleday Dell Publishing Group, Inc. Its trademark, consisting of the
words "Bantam Books" and the portrayal of a rooster, is Registered in U.S.
Patent and Trademark Office and in other countries. Marca Registrada.
Bantam Books, 666 Fifth Avenue, New York, New York 10103.

Printed in the United States of America
BVG   0   9   8   7   6   5   4   3   2   1

for
G. O. *"DOC" WATSON*,[1]
the late WILLIAM D. NEFF,[2]
the late ELIOT ELISOFON,[3]
and the late HARRY S TRUMAN,[4]
*who, when I was sixteen, encouraged me
to attempt something interesting.*

[1] Doc Watson was, during my high school years near Kansas City, the adviser to the school newspaper. Besides getting me started on writing, Doc protected me from the wrath of the football coach during my tenure as sports editor; at eighty-four, Doc is still skiing, still as skeptical as ever about what he reads in the newspapers.

[2] William D. Neff, Senior, was the publisher of the *Johnson County Herald* who employed me on a freelance basis for four years in the mid-1950s and gave me a lot of useful advice about college and career, particularly about avoiding local-boy-stays-local stagnation.

[3] Eliot Elisofon was a *Life* magazine photographer who employed me as his fetch-and-carry assistant; Elisofon's wide interests (he was also an author and a collector of art) were an inspiration, and he relentlessly pointed out to me what I'd have to do in order to prepare myself for an interesting career.

[4] Harry S Truman, over the course of several weeks as Elisofon created a photographic essay to accompany the publication of the presidential memoirs in 1955, told me a lot of stories about interesting people with an implicit "You could do that too" message. I am immortalized on the cover of *Life* as a faint shadow cast across President and Mrs. Truman as they stood in front of their home; only later, when I saw Grant Wood's painting *American Gothic*, did I realize that Elisofon had, except for my inadvertent shadow, emulated it.

Contents

Figure List

Preface

AND WHAT, MIGHT YOU ASK, IS A NEUROBIOLOGIST DOING writing a book about astronomy? I tell the astronomers that this is the neurobiologists' revenge—the astonomer Carl Sagan did, after all, write a best-selling book about neurobiology. (Indeed, *The Dragons of Eden* sets a high standard for would-be interlopers.)

Or what, for that matter, am I doing writing a book that is, in part, about shamanistic practices and the possible origins of religion? That's a little harder to answer, even to myself; unlike astronomy, such are not among my hobbies. Yet while out hiking and admiring the views from ancient ruins such as Stonehenge, I stumbled on something interesting, a candidate for how the first shaman, the first priest, the first prophet—maybe even the first scientist—might have gotten started in their part-time occupations, back in the hunter-gatherer days of the Ice Age. I have come to think of ancient astronomy as the first "knowledge-based industry," that a shaman was also likely the first scientist.

Still, I might not have gotten around to writing a book were it not for how well the discoveries illustrate something about how scientists really work (in contrast to the myths that build up). When I blunder into a series of simple discoveries that many a high school science student could have made, I am reminded that they had remained undiscovered over all those years of visitors to such sites marveling over the architecture, nearly always asking, "What was it *for?*"— but advancing no further. How does such a question ever achieve a tentative answer, susceptible to the better-known scientific processes of rationality and careful testing? We teach the rational part of science (at least to those students who go on to make up the six percent minority of the population that can pass a simple test of "scientific literacy") but we seldom manage to get across the creative process that spans the time from the first "Isn't that interesting?" to the scientific debates in learned journals. I suspect that the scientific creative process is little different from the creative process involved in writing a novel or composing a symphony.

In the seventies, I'd read the Stonehenge books of Gerald Hawkins and Fred Hoyle—and was both fascinated and dissatisfied. Surely, I thought, there must be a simpler way to predict eclipses than those clever record-keeping schemes that they were proposing. From all the examples I'd seen of emergent properties, I was well aware that complex results often arose from simple rules. Perhaps, I mused, rules for eclipse prediction could be discovered without anyone understanding why they worked.

Emergent rules is about all that this book's subject matter has to do with my usual expertise. Archaeoastronomy started out as a hobby, providing some vacation-time relief from those long days in a hot laboratory solving surgical and electronics problems, thinking how brains work, how they evolve, and what abrupt climate change does to them. Fans of my throwing theory, or the Darwin Machine, or islands in the mind, will not find them elaborated here—though "evolutionary thinking" will be found, as well as my preoccupation with climate change. As every tourist at Mesa Verde soon learns, the Anasazi disappeared due to a great drought, rather like those abrupt climate changes elsewhere that may have helped to bootstrap our apelike ancestors into more human levels of intelligence (which I discussed in *The Ascent of Mind: Ice Age Climates and the Evolution of Intelligence*).

While my earlier books have often used travels as a framework for discussing science, this one is a proper "journey of discovery." It is about formulating a question, collecting contradictory evidence, occasionally seeing how to reconcile previously unconnected evidence, revising my theory on the spot and seeking out new data, suddenly feeling that I had begun to see the world as an ancient shaman had. I did have to make one compromise: In writing for general readers, I have rearranged the order of discovery in minor ways. For example, I left the precision measurement site in the Grand Canyon until the penultimate chapter, even though it was discovered first and motivated me to look at other Anasazi sites (which, it turned out, worked very differently and required me to find a whole new way of looking at things that I'd gleaned from the initial discovery). Personally, I suspect that most good stories about scientific discoveries have also been, consciously or unconsciously, edited and rearranged to improve the telling. Scientific problems start out confused and ill-defined, with motivations that are usually different from those that develop later when the solution is unfolding. The confusion I exhibit in this book is minor, compared to what I felt!

The other rearrangement was more a matter of literary challenge than explanatory necessity. I have avoided giving the textbookish geometric explanation for eclipses (and for the northeast-to-southeast changes in sunrise and moonrise positions) in the first few chapters of the book, just to give the reader an opportunity to see how a hunter-gatherer might have approached the problem from a flat-earth viewpoint: what phenomena there were to notice, what use anyone could have made of the crude beginnings, how someone could have eventually backed into doing science without really intending to.

Emerging scientific questions are especially useful for familiarizing nonscientists with the creative aspect of science; nonscientists often feel that, unlike literature and politics, science has no place for their opinions, that it is "all fact" that they cannot debate in a familiar manner, that to create a new contribution requires unimaginable years of training. And so this is a book for those nonscientists who have always wanted to participate in a good quest, who are interested in seeing ancient ruins in a new light—and with those ruins, catching a glimpse of our pioneering ancestors who bootstrapped themselves up out of superstition.

W. H. C.
WOODS HOLE and SEATTLE

HOW THE SHAMAN
STOLE THE MOON

1

||||||||||||||||

Christopher Columbus, Master Magician

Do you believe then that the sciences would ever have arisen and become great if there had not beforehand been magicians, alchemists, astrologers and wizards, who thirsted and hungered after abscondite and forbidden powers?

FRIEDRICH NIETZSCHE, 1886

E veryone has probably wished to be present at some celebrated moment in history, just to see the surprised expressions on people's faces, to hear their murmurs and exclamations. Personally, I'd like to eavesdrop on a seldom-celebrated meeting from about 500 years ago. It's an example of a stage-managed spectacle that probably shaped the emergence of civilizations out of the hunter-gatherer life-style.

Science—and maybe religion—might have gotten its start on such an occasion. Though we think of them as somehow opposed, there once wasn't much of a difference. The beginnings of one might have marked the beginnings of the other.

ON HIS FOURTH VOYAGE TO THE NEW WORLD, CHRIS-topher Columbus got himself stranded while exploring in the Caribbean. It wasn't a navigational error: His worm-eaten ship leaked so badly that it had to be beached for repairs in what is now known as St. Anne's Bay, Jamaica. There he sat, for more than a year, impatiently awaiting the return of his lieutenant's ship with assistance.

The natives had received Columbus and his men with great kindness. But the sailors had been insubordinate earlier in the voyage, and trouble erupted once again. The sailors' lawless conduct alienated the natives, who then cut off their food supply, which made the sailors even more mutinous. How Christopher Columbus got himself out of this mess shows a genius far above his navigational skills. He carefully scheduled a meeting with the Indian chiefs just before sunset on 29 February 1504.

When they congregated, Columbus made a solemn announcement: *God didn't like the way the natives were treating Columbus and his crew. And so the Almighty had decided to remove the moon permanently, as a sign of his displeasure.*

No one records whether the natives laughed or not. Not long after this pronouncement just before sunset, the full moon peeked over the eastern horizon. The sun went down while the moon came up. The long shadows from the sunset seemed to point at the moon, as it crept onstage. Everyone's attention was focused.

Hah! It was there after all. Quite red, but still there. A buzz of conversation surely started.

Yet when it rose a little further, the voices must have momentarily quieted. Something was wrong. By the time that the moon cleared the horizon a minute later, it had become obvious to all who could see that some of the lower half of the moon was missing, a little crescent.

And over the next hour or so, more and more of the moon darkened. Finally, only a sliver was left. Then it really went dark, the dusky red moon hanging in the star-filled night sky, a ghost of its usual brilliance, surrounded by dazzling stars that were ordinarily invisible in the moon's glare.

The natives were reportedly terrified. They pleaded with Columbus to restore the moon; they would give him all the food he wanted if he would just bring back the moon.

A dramatic pause ensued. Columbus told them that he would have to retire to confer with the Almighty (said to be

an hourglass used for timing the 48-minute duration of totality!). Impatience reigned, probably including recriminations
against the chiefs who had so presumptuously cut off the
food supply.

Just before the end of the eclipse was due, Columbus
returned. He graciously announced that the Almighty had
pardoned the Indians and would allow the moon to reappear.
Sure enough, a sliver of white appeared not long afterward
on the lower edge of the dark red orb. Within the next hour
and a half, the moon was slowly restored to the natives.
Columbus's promise had come true.

Columbus probably didn't have much trouble with the
natives thereafter. Perhaps even Columbus's mutinous sailors
were duly impressed and stopped challenging their captain.
They undoubtedly reasoned that if Columbus had such a
good private line to the Almighty, heaven knows how much
more mischief he might cause.

BUT WHAT COLUMBUS HAD, LIKE THE OTHER SAILING
captains of his time, was a private line to the accumulated
wisdom of millennia of Persian, Greek, Islamic, and European science—a nautical almanac that listed the predictions
of future eclipses. Presumably Columbus used it to schedule
the meeting.

Remember that A.D. 1504 date: Whoever wrote Columbus's almanac was probably operating in ignorance of the
geometry of our solar system, those near-circular orbits and
cone-shaped shadows. Copernicus wouldn't publish his rev-
olutionary analysis of a sun-centered universe until he was
dying in 1543. Galileo died in 1642, the year that Isaac Newton was born. So that almanac from the year 1500 must have
used some empirical method to predict eclipses, perhaps a
scheme of "magic numbers" proved over the years, rather
than a scientific understanding of what was going on.

And remember the probable "mind-set" of most people
in Columbus's day. While many older Indians had probably
seen a total eclipse of the moon several times, "causing" one

was powerful magic. When someone says that something improbable is going to happen, and then it does, the effect is far different from a spontaneous occurrence. One tends to assume cause-and-effect, even today.

Columbus could hardly have been the first person to impress an audience by ordering the sun or moon to disappear, and then reappear: Clever people had probably been pulling that same stunt for millennia. Just imagine how impressive it must have been when the audience was ignorant of what we take for granted: that it's just a predictable, clockwork matter of orbits and shadows, not susceptible to human whims. But who was the first to predict an eclipse, and how did he or she figure it out?

Forecasting methods are not obvious. If a group of modern astronomers, who know all about orbits and shadow cones, was shipwrecked on an island without any reference books or computers, they probably would not know how to impress the natives with their knowledge of eclipses. However the earliest astronomer got his or her start at predicting eclipses, the method has been lost through the overlay of one improvement after another, just as people forgot how to make flint knives after metal ones became common.

Early science is unlikely to have been built on the rational application of logic, in the manner of the myth that has grown up around modern science. Logic is usually the last step, after a lot of back-and-forth fitting, in the way that a carpenter hangs a door. You can get the general drift of things by remembering that philosophy subdivided a few centuries ago into natural and religious philosophy (the latter went on to become theology), and then natural philosophy further split in the last century into natural science and what we presently call "philosophy." Looking back, these splits suggest that philosophy-religion-science were all mixed up originally—that what we call science was once part of religion, that scientists were once priests. Or vice versa. But before the priest came the shaman.

Was the first scientist a shaman, the spiritual leader of a

Stone Age band or tribe? Probably. I can see a way in which early science could have paid off quite handsomely (even without Columbus-style social manipulation), if only some simple observation was combined with supernaturalism and superstition. The payoff, strange to say, was priest-run religion.

AN OBSESSION WITH ECLIPSES COULD HAVE STARTED LONG ago, even in small bands of hunter-gatherers, long before agriculture came on the scene 12,000 years ago. How early might it have happened? Potentially, as early as we developed our obsession with the future (apes, however, have not been seen planning for tomorrow, or worrying about what the future might bring). It would have happened after we rediscovered an ancient concern with the phases of the moon.

Why pay any attention to the moon? All animals have built-in rhythms, the best known of which are the circadian rhythms: Even if we live in a deep cave without obvious clues about day and night, our bodies have cycles of activity that are about 24-25 hours long. And even if animals don't watch the moon's phases in any obvious way, their bodies often have cycles of activity that are about 28-30 days long (the menstrual cycle of women, for example), left over from ancient reproductive rhythms that synchronized mating or birth with the high tides caused by the full moon.

Besides such predispositions, the full moon is sometimes a minor spectacle—as when it sits on the eastern horizon, just before sunset, looking dusky red. The moon usually seems extra large at first appearance. For some reason, being both dusky red and sitting on the horizon makes the moon appear entirely different—enormous and strange. An hour later, when it is higher in the sky, the very same moon looks white and considerably smaller.

Occasionally, a bite gets taken out of it, later that evening—sometimes, the moon almost disappears for an hour or so, becoming a dim relic of its former self. Exaggerated reddish moonrises happen a few times each year, and

7

noticeable lunar eclipses happen more rarely, but the dramatic reddish moonrise always (clouds excepted) precedes the major spectacle of a lunar eclipse. And so we watch the full moon.

CONSIDER THE PSYCHOLOGY OF THE MOON'S DISappearances in a little more detail. We tend to associate unusual happenings with one another. And it isn't just humans: A monkey being trained to press a button that delivers food (the psychologist's version of a vending machine) is often "superstitious." If he happens to chase his tail just before pressing the button accidentally, he will sometimes chase his tail again before pressing the button intentionally ("It seems to work—why quarrel with success?" is how a human might rationalize similar behavior).

Associations are powerful. Mary Catherine Bateson once told me about being in Iran in 1978 when an earthquake occurred one evening, up on the shores of the Caspian Sea at Babolsar. The ceiling lights were swaying back and forth, and everyone ran outdoors into the night air—and that night, there was a lunar eclipse! After the memorable earthquake, the people blamed it on another part of their universe that seemed out of joint. And what had happened before this memorable night? Well, the Shah of Iran had been acting strangely, causing all manner of comment. He had actually apologized to the people for past mistakes; this conciliatory move was a most unusual happening (rulers, in their experience, acted like rulers). And it was antecedent: The Shah, they reasoned, was responsible for the earthquake! But how? Since they thought that the Shah was omnipotent, they rationalized the Shah-earthquake association in a very modern way, by postulating that he had triggered the earthquake via an underground nuclear test.

What would you do if you associated (for whatever reason) eclipses with all manner of bad luck, but were solemnly told that an eclipse was coming—and by someone who was right last time? However it got started, trying to prevent eclipses through fervent prayer, before and during an eclipse, surely must have *seemed* to work most of the time. After all,

- many of the predicted eclipses didn't happen (the methods were crude and so there were a lot of what are now called false positives); this could have led many people to believe that their prayers had prevented the eclipse; and
- many of the predicted eclipses that nonetheless happened were *partial,* allowing someone to conclude that the prayers had reversed the moon in its tracks, preventing a total eclipse.

And so prayer was powerfully reinforced because it *seemed* to work. If the priestly predictions were nearly always wrong, the announcements would have soon lost their credibility (the behavior would have "extinguished," as the psychologists like to say). If the predictions were always right (as they are today for eclipses, though not for earthquakes and such), eclipses would have lost their fascination for many people. Being right just enough of the time is what makes some situations, such as gambling, so attractive.

A control experiment, which would have omitted prayers after half of the eclipse warnings, would have shown them that the eclipse occurrence or duration was independent of their prayers. Again, priestly credibility would have suffered. But the control experiment is a recent scientific innovation, invented after scientists discovered that they were fooled too often by mere coincidence.

I can see how large groups of people would have been psychologically trapped, how *predicted* eclipses would have made them believe in the power of wishful thinking. I'm not surprised that people were fooled by *post hoc, ergo propter hoc*—the classical fallacy of "*after* this, therefore *because* of this," a fallacy that fools us every day even when we're alert to it. Despite its unreliability, one thing following another is a powerful way in which we learn our way around our environment, especially when dealing with the unfamiliar, such as a novel happening.

Partial eclipses might have gotten prayer started back before prediction was discovered. After all, every total eclipse is preceded and followed by a partial eclipse—but most eclipses are only partial. Wishful thinking during the partial phases, once the coverup starts reversing, could get the credit for the eclipse not advancing into totality. Given something (the shaman's warning) to trigger the prayers a few hours or days ahead of time, the effect seems even more powerful: Sometimes, the eclipses don't occur at all! Belief in the power of prayer to move the heavens was sure to emerge—and, of course, prediction itself would have become valued by the tribal leadership, a powerful incentive to more and better science.

Of all the early scientific discoveries we can imagine, none has the same ability as eclipse prediction to impress and manipulate large groups of people. Oft-fulfilled prophesies might convert a shaman into a full-fledged prophet, lending authority to whatever the seer had to say on other subjects. Pythagoras' theorem is important, as is Euclid's geometry, but one cannot imagine swaying a crowd with their proclamation. The scientific discovery that the earth isn't the center of the universe didn't please the crowds at all.

And eclipse forecasting would have helped the shaman with everyday matters as well. The shaman of most known hunter-gatherer tribes is supposed to be able to predict the weather, cure illness, and bring down illness upon enemies. Given the strength of the placebo effect (the power of suggestion alone seems to work for one out of three pain sufferers), one can easily imagine that a shaman who had just manipulated the moon or sun would have even more success than usual at relieving pain.

Even if the tribal leadership was blind to the Columbus-style possibilities for manipulation, even if the healers didn't know about eclipses, a fortune-teller could still have made a good living from eclipse forecasting. We humans seem to have an inordinate appetite for predictions about what the future might bring. While eclipses might be unrelated to "You will meet a dark stranger" and other such staples of the repertoire, a fortune-teller's ability to predict an eclipse would be a powerful validation of her or his abilities. (If she's right about the moon disappearing for an hour, then surely she has a powerful pipeline to the spirits—and maybe we'd better make her a nice gift.)

So while this is a limited story about how predictive science *might* have originated via imperfect methods, it may also be one of the stories about how primitive religions arose and were sustained by their apparent success in predicting or manipulating the heavens. That potential priming of the human belief system is of far more significance than eclipses themselves. The social organization provided by religion has been of vast importance in human evolution, though we have no idea how far back the religious impulse goes (still, no one has seen apes holding prayer breakfasts). Did predictive science start a million years ago in prehuman days, or in our hunter-gatherer days of the last Ice Age, or with our big agricultural civilizations of the last 6,000 years? Or just among Euclid's geometric predecessors in ancient Greece, maybe 2,600 years ago?

Given the invention of eclipse forecasting, I have no trouble imagining an almost-modern form of mass religion with its belief in the efficacy of wishful thinking (and, while prayer may not move the moon, it's still mentally useful) and the emergence of powerful leaders with specialized knowledge. Those early leaders may have been the shamans who seemed to have such power over the sun and moon because they'd figured out a method of eclipse prediction—and likely kept it a secret among themselves.

Asking about the origins of eclipse prediction isn't merely an attempt to understand one of the great spectacles of nature, or just an attempt to understand the origins of religion or fortune-telling or early astronomy-astrology-cosmology, fascinating as they are. It is also an attempt to understand how science got started.

The intellectual challenge faced by the earliest scientists was enormous, trying to take the first steps without scientific predecessors. What was the tradition they operated within, what led up to this discovery of how to predict eclipses?

Newton was not the first of the age of reason. He was the last of the magicians, the last of the Babylonians and Sumerians, the last great mind which looked out on the visible and intellectual world with the same eyes as those who began to build our intellectual inheritance rather less than 10,000 years ago.

JOHN MAYNARD KEYNES, 1942

2

||||||||||||||

How Does
Stonehenge Work?

[*The stones of Stonehenge*] *are as prodigious as
any tales I ever heard of them, and worth going
this journey to see. God knows what their use
was!*

SAMUEL PEPYS, Diary, 11 June 1668

Pilgrims to Stonehenge may call themselves tourists these days, I thought as I drove along the valley in Salisbury Plain, but I felt more like a pilgrim myself. The paved highway overlies a well-worn footpath from pilgrimages past. To the ancient traveler, not having been prepared by picture postcards or television specials, the first sight of upright stones in the distance must have been particularly intriguing.

Their size is hard to judge, lacking adjacent trees to which you might compare a stone's height. That some of the upright stones are capped by bridging stones is obvious, even from the distance. And they were once extensively capped, huge lintels hoisted aloft and carefully positioned, creating a stone circle in the sky. As you get closer to Stonehenge and begin to see people in the vicinity, you realize just how tall the stones are. To the ancient pilgrim, not accustomed to multistory buildings, they probably seemed enormous as well as exotic.

I suspect that the pilgrims had to stop and prepare themselves before entering the ancient precincts, just as I had to stand in line for the opportunity to contribute a few coins to

the present government of the island. At least the ancient
pilgrims didn't have to walk under a highway and then hike
up out of a tunnel before approaching the now-silent stage.

In its beginning the site was a simple, circular earthwork or "henge," an open space bordered by a chalk
bank and large enough to hold several hundred people.
Outside the entrance stood a weather-roughened stone,
the well-known Heel Stone. For a thousand years, forty
or more unremembered generations, this earthwork
continued to be the meeting-place of native farmers,
unaltered except for the digging-out of a circle of pits,
the Aubrey Holes, just within the banks.

Then, as late as 2200 BC, people brought some
Welsh bluestones to the site, started to set them up in
two circles, one inside the other, and constructed an
avenue, undeviatingly straight, up the northern hillside
towards the henge's entrance. Abruptly the work
stopped. The bluestones were removed and in their
place dozens of massive sarsens were dragged a score of
heavy miles from the Marlborough Downs. A
horseshoe-shaped setting of five archways, the tri-
lithons, was erected. Around it, enclosing it in a ring of
dark stone, the pillars of the outer circle were raised,
lintels lifted and laid along their tops. . . Later, the bluestones were restored, set up in a circle, dismantled,

16

arranged differently. . . . The work gangs eventually
gave up 2000 years after their ancestors had begun. . . .
AUBREY BURL, *The Stonehenge People*, 1987

I heard people marveling at the engineering feats, saying
the same things as do the crowds surrounding the pyramids
of Egypt. Stonehenge was built about the same time, almost
five thousand years ago, long before wheels and cranes and
hydraulic lifts. Those big upright sarsen stones had to be
hauled in from Marlborough Downs (and there is a major
river valley to descend and ascend). The smaller bluestones
were transported from far beyond the distant western horizons: They come from the Preseli Mountains in southwest
Wales. While glaciers might have carried along the stones and
scattered them hereabouts, the traditional assumption is that
the Stonehenge builders barged them most of the way. In
either eventuality, they had to be hauled uphill to Stonehenge. Why build here? Why not build your ceremonial
center down near the banks of the River Avon, between the
plateau of Salisbury Plain and that of Marlborough Downs?

Perhaps this site was chosen because the view is better
up here. This area is called Salisbury Plain, but it isn't exactly
flat. The "plain" has a number of deep depressions created by
the water runoff over the millennia, which has cut down into
the chalk bedrock that lies just beneath a surface layer of soil
and grass. The roads seem to follow the grooves. And so the
traveler's view can be limited until one is close enough to
Stonehenge to make out some of the details, such as those
lintels. As you arrive at Stonehenge, your obstructed view
expands. It extends without limit to all horizons, though not
really like the view from a mountain top—I was reminded of
being at sea, flat horizons all around (give or take a wave or
two), and no obstructions except those big, exotic stones.

One reason that you can see so far is that the chalk
underneath the thin layer of surface soil isn't very hospitable
to tree roots. Indeed, the subsurface chalk is why these stones
are still standing. Many sarsens have stayed upright all these

millennia because the builders dug foundation holes into the chalk, rather like sockets for teeth, in which to seat the stones. That makes them hard to topple, though many a stonemason in search of nice raw material has tried to quarry at Stonehenge over the years. They occasionally succeeded, which is why so much of Stonehenge is missing. If the authorities were to permit you to walk around probing the ground with a fencing foil after some heavy rains, you'd discover a number of places where you could sink it in, up to the hilt (usually, you'd encounter the hard chalk within a knife's length). Over a hundred such empty stone sockets are hidden from view beneath the grass.

Some of them form rings around the central collection. There is a ring of 30 so-called "Z Holes" and, just outside it, another ring of 30 "Y Holes." Farther out, just inside the bank, is a ring of smaller stones, older than the others. Those 56 "Aubrey Holes" were named for John Aubrey, the seventeenth-century explorer of Stonehenge.

Stonehenge is surrounded by a low earthen bank, beyond which is a ditch. Hardly large enough to qualify as a moat, the ditch is difficult to see anymore. Several large stones are outside the ditch perimeter in the northeast, such as the "Heel Stone." The "Avenue" leading to these outlying stones is bordered by its own bank and ditch, but it was a late addition.

In between the few modern trees on the horizon (analysis of ancient pollen suggests that there used to be many more), you see some odd-shaped mounds, especially to the north. They too are human in construction, and about as old as the earliest Stonehenge—in the vicinity of 5,000 years old.

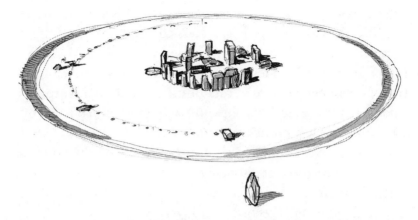

Simply nothing else around the countryside fixes your eye; this isn't like the ancient Greek temples, situated to impress the visitor by the vistas they command as well as by the view seen by the visitor looking at the temple from the approach path. What made the view here so worthwhile?

MAYBE THE ANCIENT BUILDERS INSTEAD LIKED THE view of the *night* skies. It is often suspected that the heavens were much closer to the interests of our ancient ancestors, back when after-dark entertainments were more restricted.

Yet the view of the heavens would have been almost as good from down by the river's edge. Getting rid of minor low-lying obstructions usually isn't worth it, as the stars near the horizon are already obscured by that extra-long path through the atmosphere. Building Stonehenge down near the River Avon would have avoided the long haul for both the stones and the drinking water. And avoided the wind.

Maybe the view was part of the scene-setting for ceremony, the way that Delphi has long views from its cliff-edge sites. But here the view (outside of Stonehenge itself) seems unexceptional to me, certainly little different from other places around Salisbury Plain.

One possibility that remains is that the view was for doing science. Stonehenge has somehow become the universally recognized symbol of scientific sophistication in prehistoric times, just as the caves at Lascaux, Niaux, and Altamira have become the symbols of Ice Age sophistication in art. The 25,000-year-old cave art tends to speak for itself, however; the 5,000-year-old Stonehenge does not. We have a rather superficial understanding of how those stones functioned. Were they useful in cataloging the heavens? Keeping a calendar? Or predicting eclipses, a step on the road to saving Christopher Columbus's skin?

Whose eyes should we attempt to see through? If we are to attempt to look at Stonehenge through the eyes of the earliest scientists, how far back should we go? Instead of thinking in terms of record-keeping agricultural civilizations such as Sumer or Babylon, perhaps we need to try to see the world through the eyes of the hunter-gatherers who preceded them, or those of the early agriculturalists who first settled down in one place. The hunter-gatherer societies of today are notably supernaturalistic in their approach to natural phenomena; if they are any indication of what a prehistoric society thought like, an eclipse prediction scheme that worked only half of the time would probably have been a great success, because of feeding on wishful thinking. I doubt that our ancestors had our modern attitudes regarding how good a scientific explanation needs to be in order to be judged successful.

AS I WALK AROUND STONEHENGE, I LOOK BETWEEN the stones. Whenever two stones line up, I sight along their edges. If I use the right side of one stone, and the left side of a more distant stone, the view becomes needle thin, pointing a well-defined direction. Gunsights tend to use grooves and needles, but the two opposing edges may have been the early version of defining a sightline. And where do such sightlines point? At Stonehenge, they merely point to different places on the distant horizon, none of which seem (to me) to be very interesting.

At least, those places on the horizon are not very interesting in the middle of the day, when Stonehenge is open to visitors. Were I here at sunrise, wandering among the long

shadows, peering through reddish-tinged stones, I might see the sun framed at the end of my sightline. But that would occur only on certain days, such as the shortest day of the year in late December—which, for reasons that I will avoid elaborating upon, is also when sunrise reaches its extreme position on the southeastern horizon. The sun turns around the next day and, with each successive sunrise, heads back north.

Another interesting day is the longest day of the year in late June, when the sun turns around from its northeastern extreme. Actually, the view of the sunrise remains the same for a week or more, as the day-to-day movement in the sun's position on the horizon alters very slowly at those times of the year (that's why they are called the winter and summer solstices, *solstice* deriving from the Latin for the "sun standing" still). Halfway between the solstices, near the equinoxes in March and September, the place where the sun rises virtually gallops from day to day, jumping more than a full sun diameter along the horizon from one morning to the next, leaving space in between untouched by rising sun.

Other Stonehenge sightlines are to the extreme sunset positions in the southwest and northwest. And there are some to extreme positions of moonrise and moonset. The moon isn't often seen at the end of such sightlines, since the moon's cycle is close to 18.61 years long. (Why? The "precession of the nodes" of the moon's tilted orbit takes that long to complete. Rounded up, it's 19 years; three such cycles are about 56 years.)

> This island . . . is situated in the north, and is inhabited by the Hyperboreans, who are called by that name because their home is beyond the point whence the north wind (Boreas) blows; and the land is both fertile and productive of every crop, and since it has an unusually temperate climate it produces two harvests each year. . . . The account is also given that the god visits the islands every nineteen years, the period in which the return of the stars to the same place in the heavens is

accomplished; and for this reason the nineteen-year period is called by the Greeks the "year of Meton."

> the ancient Greek historian
> HECATAEUS, ca. 500 B.C.

SIGHTLINES CREATED BY THE STONES ARE THE CONVEN-
tional "explanation" of the Stonehenge architectural plan; the
first such suggestion was made four centuries ago, noting that
the Avenue to the outlying Heel Stone was also the observation path to sunrise for the longest day of the year. Indeed, we now know that many megalithic monuments
around the British Isles can function in a similar manner. What
makes Stonehenge special is the claim of various archae-
ologically inclined astronomers that the Stonehenge architecture was used to predict eclipses of the sun and moon, that
Stonehenge "functions" by design as a neolithic computer.

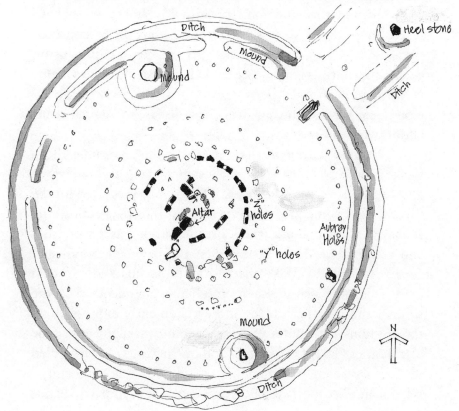

Astronomers and historians usually assume that record-keeping was the way that the secret of eclipses was discovered. They carefully noted the cycles of the moon, how they correspond with the eclipses of moon and sun, and then they noted that eclipses repeat on a cycle of 6585.3 days (the *Saros* cycle of 18 years and 11 days). By extrapolating ahead, one should be able to predict the dates of future eclipses from the record of past ones.

The three complicated eclipse–prediction schemes for Stonehenge all focus on this eclipse repeat cycle, all use those 56 Aubrey Holes in the ring that surrounds (and antedates) the central megaliths. Fred Hoyle's complicated eclipse-prediction scheme for Stonehenge focuses on this eclipse repeat cycle, using those 56 Aubrey holes in the ring that surrounds (and antedates) the central megaliths. He hypothesizes several movable markers, transferred from stone to stone around the ring (and presumably heavy enough to resist mischievous youths and strong winds for 56 consecutive years). One "counts down" to the next eclipse, using such a computing scheme. Gerald Hawkins's original scheme is much more simple; he suggested that the Stonehenge astronomers were counting off eclipse "seasons" which recur about every six months.

The only hard evidence for any of the intriguing theories are those 56 holes in the earliest stone ring at Stonehenge and 19 in one of the later ones. They're not predicted by the theory, only some of the many assumptions that go into the theory. And so many learned disputes among archaeologists and astronomers have appeared in the pages of *Nature* and *Science*, trying to make the most of the unavoidably thin evidence. In science as elsewhere, there is a tendency that, the thinner the evidence is, the more vehemently expressed are the opinions. One of the early archaeological criticisms of the astronomer Gerald Hawkins's book *Stonehenge Decoded* called it "tendentious, arrogant, slipshod and unconvincing," which, in retrospect, it has proved not to be. In particular, it provided a big surprise: The Stonehenge people were observing the moon's horizon cycle, as well as the sun's.

Those 56-year schemes are complicated enough that even someone with my training in spherical trigonometry and astronomy has to study them for a while before they begin to make sense. I cannot imagine trying to explain them to someone else without the aid of some complicated three-dimensional diagrams showing the orbit of the moon around the earth, and of the earth-moon combination around the sun. Someone, somewhere, likely used one of those three schemes involving 56-year-long record keeping, even if it turns out that the operators of Stonehenge didn't. Surely these complicated schemes are not stumbled into, just by accident—which is why I think that they are candidates for some *intermediate* stage in astronomy, but not an early one. How did eclipse prediction get started? Maybe with a method that only worked some of the time, but using simple observations, simple record keeping, simple reasoning?

RETRACING MY STEPS THROUGH THE UNDERPASS, I RE-flected that whether or not the Stonehenge priests actually accomplished eclipse prediction, it is clear that, at some stage, various other peoples did. For example, the Greek philosopher Thales somehow predicted the 585 B.C. solar eclipse—and the Babylonian astronomers seemed to know a lot about eclipses (though lacking a geometrical model).

Even the natives of the Americas, probably isolated from any Eurasian protoscience for more than 10,000 years, managed to predict eclipses. And the evidence for the New World people doing it is better than that for the Old World peoples: The Dresden Codex (which is made of bark, not porcelain) is named for the German museum where the painted text now resides, and it is one of only about four sizable examples of Mayan writing found in Mexico that survived the Catholic priests. Once its inscriptions were deciphered and analyzed, it became apparent that the Maya knew all about eclipses of the sun. This table, covering the period A.D. 755-788, didn't miss a single one of the 77 partial or total solar eclipses of that period.

So were the Maya great observers, compiling a "Mayan Almanac" from extensive eyewitness accounts? No. Only four of those 77 solar eclipses could have been observed in Mexico and, however good their communications system, it could not have been good enough: Some of the listed eclipses were visible only in Antarctica. And most partial solar eclipses are never noticed. So this "Mayan Almanac" is a worldwide *prediction* table, not a list of *observations.* The Maya knew the sun-moon cycles well enough to be alert for an eclipse, even though they probably didn't know where on earth it would be seen.

The Dresden Codex can be interpreted to predict about 98 percent of lunar eclipses as well. This near-perfection suggests that the Codex was probably designed for solar eclipses, and that another bark record existed, since lost (or burned by the pious Spaniards), specifically for predicting lunar eclipses. With the appropriate corrections, the Dresden Codex can even be made to work to predict modern eclipses: If those shipwrecked modern astronomers had a tourist replica of that ancient Mayan bark text, they too could predict eclipses without a reference library.

BUT THIS IS SURELY NOT HOW PREDICTING ECLIPSES got started, I reflected while driving north on the road up to another megalithic monument. Less than an hour north of Stonehenge by modern highway, Avebury was a long day's journey for the ancient pilgrim. It is atop another chalky landscape called the Marlborough Downs; the pilgrim would have had to hike down into the Vale of Pewsey, across the River Avon, and then back uphill. The pilgrims probably stopped at enormous man-made mounds along the way such as Silbury Hill.

From any one island, solar eclipses are often 400-800 years apart. Even if you have widespread communications so that word of distant solar eclipses reaches you, you would have to keep careful records for a long time in order to discover the repeat patterns. Yet most civilizations are fragile. Uprisings destroy the orderly records of events; plagues kill off the scribes; religious and philosophical differences frequently cause records to be destroyed. The priests accompanying the Spanish explorers are regularly cursed by scholars for burning nearly all of the Mayan books written on folded bark. (They were, of course, probably worried about accusations of being "soft on pagan religions" by their local chapter of the Inquisition.)

Knowledgeable people were lost as well. The earliest recorded solar eclipse was probably the one of 22 October, 2134 B.C. Ancient Chinese records note that "the Sun and Moon did not meet harmoniously." The two Chinese royal astronomers, Hsi and Ho, failed to predict it and were executed by the unhappy emperor. Other major, long-lasting civilizations such as ancient Egypt and medieval Europe sometimes didn't record a single mention of eclipses. This suggests that eclipses might have been too sacred to mention. While an oral tradition among the select few is one good way to keep the eclipse prediction method secret, it also makes it possible to lose the secret if several people die suddenly.

Record keeping—a table of observations of eclipses—has to be pretty good before it is of much use for eclipse prediction. Gaps in a record can be a big problem unless one knows exactly how long the hiatus was. When comparing records from different observers, one also needs a universal calendar so that a "date" truly represents the same day in both locations. We have enough trouble converting from the Julian to our Gregorian calendar; it was even worse in Roman days when a complicated moon-based calendar was in style. Voltaire once quipped that, while the Roman generals always won, they never knew what day it was when the victory occurred. Back in the Dark Ages, scribes lost track of a year every now and then, which is why the birth of Jesus is now placed in about 6 B.C. The time of year also seems to have been moved from springtime back to a few days after the winter solstice.

Perhaps there is another early method for predicting eclipses aside from historical records, with the observation table coming later as record keeping became better, after which someone figured out the repetition cycle. Perhaps the tables merely codified the knowledge that built up from the careful attention paid to eclipses, thanks to the successes of a more primitive prediction method. But what is that method, if the modern astronomers can't figure it out?

Recognizing that lunar eclipses only occurred at the full moon, when moonrise occurs near sunset, was likely the first step. Perhaps the new moon was similarly known as a danger period for solar eclipses. Eclipses simply never occur when the moon is waxing or waning. Surely in the months following a lunar eclipse, each full moon was carefully watched.

THE PICTURE POSTCARDS SHOW AVEBURY AS A GREAT circle, with a high earthen bank. Unlike Stonehenge, Avebury has an *inner* ditch (which rather detracts from the notion that these ditches were protective moats). Avebury is several city blocks in diameter, and the aerial views make it look like some sort of prehistoric particle accelerator buried in the earth. But its high circular bank is now split in four places to accommodate modern roads; there is, incredibly, a crossroads pub in the middle of the Avebury circle, and an adjacent village that has obliterated part of the great bank-and-ditch in recent centuries.

In each "quadrant" created by the roads, upright stones are seated in chalk sockets. Indeed, the Avebury stones often look like incisors, bicuspids, and molars. Marlborough Downs, too, is underlain by chalk. So is much of England, as one can see at those white cliffs of Dover.

The Avebury stones march along in stately procession—too far apart to be bridged by lintels, in the Stonehenge fashion. Two small rings of stones are in the center of the large Avebury circle but, unlike the concentric rings at Stone-

Avebury stones (*left*) and the deep ditch and its correspondingly tall bank. Hikers at right provide some sense of scale.

henge, these small rings are adjacent. Like Stonehenge, there are no obvious sightlines at Avebury—or rather there are too many, with so many stones that the lines between them serve to point a great many directions. Even if a few should point to a solstice or a lunar extreme, what are all the others for? To disguise the purpose of the few?

Whoever finds significance in a selected sightline may simply be imposing his own preconceptions on the place—it helps believability if there are only a few sightlines and most are sun or lunar extremes. Stonehenge has at least ten such sightlines among its earliest stones, including the particularly obvious major axis through the Heel Stone in the direction of summer solstice sunrise; if you use the more modern stones, they provide Stonehenge sightlines in every which direction, not just the extreme positions of sun and moon on the horizon. So too at Avebury—sightlines to everywhere.

The size of Avebury and its many arcs of stately stones make one realize that Stonehenge once had stones in those Aubrey Holes. And that Stonehenge too had a significant bank and ditch surrounding it. The bank at Avebury is several stories high above the bottom of the ditch, far higher than anything at Stonehenge. Remaining sections of the bank can appear level and so the viewer standing near the central stones is treated to an artificially leveled horizon, one that obscures the distant hills and trees that might create irregularities in the perceived horizon. Was that an intended function of the bank, to smooth the observer's horizon by elevating it a little?

Exhibit A: A smooth horizon. For what is it so handy?

ANOTHER MOMENT IN PREHISTORY UPON WHICH I would happily eavesdrop would be the first time that someone watching an eclipse of the moon said, "Aren't these happening awfully often? When was the last eclipse? It wasn't all that long ago." And so people would have argued about the previous eclipse, correcting one another with examples of the events associated with each of the recent full moons. Exactly how often might a diligent observer see another eclipse?

I puzzled over this while flying home, and finally realized that there was a way to answer this question without undertaking years of observation. On my way to the physics-astronomy library is one of the most impressive of modern sightlines: a pedestrian walkway and parkland on a northwest-southeast axis downhill through the University of Washington's campus. It points to Mount Rainier. In Seattle, when one sees an elongated open space, one automatically looks at the horizon to see if the great white volcano is visible through the clouds. I suppose that's why I was disappointed with the horizon at Stonehenge: a vista with a missing view.

I sat down near the library windows with some big books from Vienna that list all of the eclipses since 2,002 B.C. Though called the "canons," they aren't great leather-bound tomes in Germanic typefaces but rather softbound computer printouts. They list nearly 20,000 eclipses—so where does one start? First I picked a region where the observers might have lived: one place is as good as another, as far as seeing eclipses is concerned (clouds excepted!). Since I'm interested in the Anasazi of the American Southwest about A.D. 700 for other reasons, I picked that time and place. Then I started entering the lunar and solar eclipses into my laptop computer—not all of them, just the eclipses that they might have seen then and there.

I got tired of this after 125 years, so I tabulated the statistics. During the period between A.D. 700 and 824, an observer could have seen as many as 56 total and 57 partial lunar eclipses. There were 14 solar eclipses where more than half of the solar disk was obscured. You don't usually notice a partial solar eclipse, so I only counted the occasions where totality occurred nearby; I was assuming that rumors of a total eclipse will spread a few hundred miles to my hypothetical observer in the Four Corners (where the modern states of Arizona, New Mexico, Colorado, and Utah meet).

This means that about one potentially observable eclipse occurs in an "average year." However, as I noticed scanning down my list, eclipses are not evenly distributed: Sometimes a series of three or four eclipses can be seen in a two-year period; other times, no eclipses can be observed for about four years. So they cluster. There was often a second lunar eclipse on the sixth full moon after the first. Now, wasn't that nice!

If moonrise is carefully watched for a partial eclipse ending, the vigil maintained all night while most people sleep, and moonset watched near sunrise the next morning for signs of a partial eclipse beginning, the diligent observer would see many more eclipses than seen by the modern evening-only spectator. Given such diligent observers and unclouded viewing conditions, one gets a 56 percent chance of another lunar eclipse at the sixth full moon after an eclipse, an 11 percent chance at the twelfth, 8 percent at the seventeenth, and 5 percent at the eighteenth. If cloudiness or sleepiness causes the observer to miss an eclipse at the sixth full moon, the eclipse interval may appear to be twelve instead.

Surely a second lunar eclipse within a year of another would be cause for some observers to discuss when the previous one occurred, counting backward to discover that it had been either six or twelve full moons ago. And so the sixth and the twelfth full moon after an eclipse could readily get the reputation of being particular danger periods. *Count to six, and then count to six again.*

Too bad we only have five fingers, you say? Contrary to the usual decimal notions, one can readily count to six and twelve on the fingers. On the sixth full moon, you close down those five extended fingers and clench your fist. On the seventh, you pick up the count on the other hand, extending one finger—and so on to two clenched fists upon the twelfth full moon. That makes the full moons coinciding with a clenched fist the "dangerous ones," threatening to disappear.

About 67 percent of all lunar eclipses occur at either the sixth or twelfth full moon following an observed eclipse, so by itself the clenched fist method is going to work two-thirds of the time. However, when no eclipses have been observed for a year, it gets slightly more complicated. While lunar eclipses do occur on the later multiples of six (18, 24, 30, etc.), many occur a month earlier than that (17, 23, 29, 35, and 53 months for the A.D. 700–824 lunar eclipses). Such eclipse intervals longer than a year account for 33 percent of the total; simply treating the late eclipse-danger periods as two months wide (17-18, 23-24, etc.) will encompass essentially all cases.

Solar eclipses, I discovered from the canons, also occur on the same six-month spacing as the lunar eclipses. They're just a half-month earlier or later than the lunar eclipse danger zone, occurring at the new moon that precedes or follows the full moon eclipse alert. But solar eclipses are reported (on my mostly covered criterion, word traveling a few hundred miles) about eight times less frequently. And probably even less so; this fraction, unlike the one for lunar eclipses, probably varies with the particular century and observation site. Thus you need not get started on *solar* eclipse prediction by observing one solar eclipse and counting new moons thereafter. You can get synchronized by observing even a partial *lunar* eclipse, counting by sixes (and making allowances after a year of no eclipses), and watching out for the new moons that precede and follow the lunar eclipse alerts. Because of this lunar-to-solar linkage, *learning to predict commonly observed lunar eclipses was likely the path of discovery for solar eclipse prediction*.

So eclipse prediction is potentially quite easy, so long as you can be wrong half of the time. And the beliefs associated with intermittent reinforcement suggest that being wrong occasionally is, paradoxically, a psychological advantage.

This clenched-fist counting scheme is uncomplicated, easy to discover (I may have discovered it with the aid of modern computers, but anyone curious about when the last eclipse happened could have guessed the rule within a few years), and even easier to operate over the years.

Of course, I mused (when the excitement of discovery wore off), solar and lunar extremes on the horizon have nothing to do with my counting-by-sixes eclipse prediction scheme. Nor do movable-marker 56-hole counting schemes. Indeed, clenched-fist doesn't need horizon observations at all, certainly not the artificially flattened horizon that so impressed me at Avebury. Ironically, I've "explained" something without using *any* of the pieces of the puzzle that anyone has identified, thus far.

But having found one simple scheme for predicting eclipses, I am led to ask: Are there other simple schemes? Could equally simple schemes make use of observations of the sun and moon sitting on a flat horizon, of the sort that the Stonehenge builders made—and so immortalized in its architecture?

Anyone who has lived
through an English winter
can see the point
of building Stonehenge
to make the sun come back.

the ethologist ALISON JOLLY, 1988

3

||||||||||||||||

Picturing the Eclipsed Sun with a Holy Leaf

Between the idea
And the reality
Between the motion
And the act
Falls the Shadow.

T. S. ELIOT,
"The Hollow Men," 1925

Totality. The very word brings up an image of an eerie scene, accompanied by paradoxical phrases such as "darkness at noon." The total solar eclipse is usually a once-in-a-lifetime event for the person lucky enough to see it at all. Everyone who gets to see a total solar eclipse also gets to see a partial eclipse, the process of the moon slowly covering up the sun and then slowly uncovering it. Most people, however, get to see *only* a partial eclipse because they aren't in the 160-mile-wide path of the moon's shadow: the moon only partly covers the sun before reversing, when you aren't in the path of totality.

When the moon doesn't quite manage to obscure the sun, the eclipse is hard to see, even if you know that it is going to happen and are alert for it. Even a crescent sun can be too bright to look at. The only partial solar eclipse that I've ever viewed directly happened to occur just before sunset, as the sun and the new moon together sank lower and lower into the western sky, and finally into the Olympic Mountains as viewed from Seattle.

You can sometimes study the sun's shape just before it sets, if you are careful. The sun's brightness is dimmed by the long path taken by the light through the atmosphere; sometimes it becomes dim enough to allow a brief glimpse. That evening, as the sun neared the horizon, the moon could be seen just in front of it, obscuring the sun's lower left. The three-dimensionality was quite striking. The moon was, literally, backlit. You could see how the notion that "the moon did it" would have arisen as an explanation for solar eclipses, even though the new moon is ordinarily invisible in the sun's glare for a day or two.

The sun is too bright (and too dangerous) to view when higher in the sky. Observers rarely study its shape. Should the partial eclipse occur in the middle of the day, the sky may darken only about as much as if some high overcast had dimmed the sun a little—and then, because you are seldom in the path of totality, the sunshine brightens again, just as if the high cloud had drifted away. Hardly a big occasion. The important thing about viewing partial solar eclipses is that you can get an hour's warning of the potentially frightening totality.

ANY FAN OF ECLIPSES HAS HEARD OF PINHOLE CAMeras, which use a hole in a card to produce an inverted image of the eclipsing sun on a screen. Pinhole images are far easier to produce than you might think; you don't need a darkened tent with a hole in the roof, plus a nice white surface for a screen. Pinhole images occur in nature, as you can discover lounging in the shade of a tree whose leaves have been perforated by insects. Likely, someone remembered those little round spots of light that had inexplicably turned into crescents before the world darkened. Odd-shaped spots, all facing the same way, are certainly striking, evoking a sense of warped reality. Even if you can't articulate what's different, you feel as if "something is happening."

If you are watching for a solar eclipse, just hold a perforated leaf at arm's length toward the sun, the way that a child instinctively does to backlight an autumn leaf. Look down at your chest to the leaf's shadow—and see the little crescent of

light in the midst of the
shadow. The leaf is probably
the world's first portable pinhole camera. As you move the
leaf farther away, the light
spot changes from the shape
of the insect's hole to the
shape of the eclipsing sun.
The smaller the hole, the
sharper the image.

Once you get the idea
that the hole's the thing, you
may no longer require the assistance of a leaf-cutting insect or a plant species with
naturally perforated leaves, such as the philodendron species
commonly called Swiss Cheese. Just punch a hole with a
twig. Or, if leafless, merely cross your fingers (for good
luck?) to produce a small opening and inspect your hand's
shadow for a little crescent.

I almost didn't see the midday eclipse in Seattle that got
me started on nonstandard pinhole methods; the path of totality was over Canada, and the calculations showed that it would
be less than half-total in Seattle. Furthermore, at the hour of
the eclipse, it was overcast in Seattle, though the sun seemed
on the verge of reappearing from behind a high, thin layer of
moisture. I peeked through the window shades of a south-
facing window, and thought the prospects of seeing anything
quite poor. The clouds were so bright that I couldn't even distinguish the sun, much less its shape. Yet the sun was casting
modest shadows of the window frame across the desktop.

Then I noticed the spots of light on the ceiling. Obviously, they were reflections of the sunlight, off of something
on the desktop. The spots moved—ah, my wristwatch was
reflecting the sunlight. I tried covering the crystal face of the
watch with two fingers, and the large, round spot on the
ceiling disappeared.

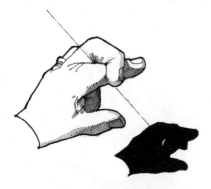

Yet the small ones remained. And they seemed crescent-shaped. Nothing was crescent-shaped on my watch. I tried covering each little shiny patch of chrome at the bracket where the wrist strap attaches. And the crescent on the ceiling suddenly disappeared.

The chrome patch was a small rectangle, not crescent. And then it finally dawned on me: The crescent on the ceiling is the shape of the sun when partially eclipsed. Even though I couldn't see the sun looking out the window because the nearby clouds seemed so bright, the image was amazingly sharp. The chrome rectangle was simply acting like a pinhole camera, combined with a mirror.

Once I had the idea (one that has probably been invented by many a school teacher over the years, trying to keep the children from looking directly at the sun), I took off the watch and propped it up on the desk, repositioning it so as to lower the crescent from the ceiling to the far wall of the room, where it was darker. Now I could walk up to the wall, take off my glasses, and closely examine the crescent. The nick that the moon had taken out of the sun was quite visible. Over the course of the next hour, it changed; the sun was never more than half-covered before the nick began to retreat.

I had some time to play around with the size of the mirror. When I used a small rectangular mirror, borrowed from my wife's purse, I only saw a rectangle on the wall. Similarly, when I used a small dental mirror, I saw only a round spot and not the crescent shape of the partially eclipsed sun. I used some bandage tape to mask most of the little mirror, leaving only a small hole unobscured. And finally the crescent shape appeared on the wall. The size of that facet on my watch seemed just about right, close enough to a pinhole for the shape to be that of the light source, rather than the reflector.

Crystals, at least those with many small-but-flat reflecting surfaces, also ought to be useful for viewing eclipses; a small facet serves to combine the pinhole with a mirror. Pull the shades except for a small opening, lay your crystal or jewel on the windowsill in the sunlight, and walk up to inspect the crescent spots reflected onto the walls. A square millimeter seems about the area needed for a mirror to function as a pinhole; little spangles embedded in a plaster wall would work nicely. A cave with a ray of sunlight coming in the smokehole, touching a shiny piece of mica, could have been the first movie theater, entertainment for the dozens—if you don't mind giving away your secret of eclipse forecasting.

Either leaf or crystal or crossed fingers would allow an alarm for a total solar eclipse, were this technique routinely used during the day of the new moon. The knowledgeable would likely warn the others to start praying. It's another entry-level eclipse forecasting method, simple enough not to require planning or antecedent techniques. It gives an hour's *warning* of possible totality rather than the many-months-ahead *prediction* of the counting-by-sixes clenched fist method.

So eclipse Method #2 might be called the "Holy Leaf" or "Crossed Fingers." And the crystal (or jewel or piece of broken mica) is its slightly harder-to-discover corollary. Since prehistoric peoples probably wouldn't have understood the principle by which the holy leaf and the crystal were related, I suppose that I'd better just call it Method #3 ("The Crystal"), rather than merely a corollary, since they were likely to be discovered independently of one another.

Since that day with the wristwatch, each time that I've been in a cathedral observing rays of sunshine illuminating a jeweled altarpiece, I've wondered if the architecture and the jewel facets were influenced by an ancient practice of just that sort.

41

WHY DO WE CALL THEM NEW MOONS, ANYWAY? I can see why the first little crescent seen after sunset might be called new, but new moon on your calendar is an astronomical abstraction. You can't see them; there's a night or two when no thin crescent of moon can be seen (because of the sun's glare near sunrise, and then sunset), then the moon reappears above sunset.

But prehistoric peoples concerned about eclipses might find the exact day of new moon just as "real" as the day of full moon. Nothing may ordinarily happen on the exact day of the new moon, but solar eclipses occasionally happen. If you're aware that something might happen during the daytime when the moon can no longer be seen at twilight, new moon might be a significant time of the month, when a careful watch has to be kept with a crystal or holy leaf or crossed fingers. "Good luck" might be the avoidance of a solar eclipse.

WINDOWS IN A ROCK WALL ARE ONE OF THE MORE spectacular features of the canyon country. They do not, alas, qualify as pinholes in most cases. Rock arches are the most graceful forms, one of the nicest being Delicate Arch at Arches National Park north of Moab, Utah.

The first time that I hiked up to see it was on a summer evening. Delicate Arch is situated on the rim of a giant bowl, almost a funnel, carved in the sandstone. The arch itself rises, crests gracefully at about four stories high, and then drops like a Roman column to rest on a little pedestal, a platform of sorts on the edge of the bowl: Imagine a delicate V-shaped coffee cup whose finger loop has been displaced to the top of the cup's rim. Beyond the edge of the bowl, the rock drops away steeply into a little valley, on the far side of which is the end-of-the-road viewpoint from which most visitors look up to view Delicate Arch. But they miss seeing the bowl, on whose edge the arch seems suspended.

I sat atop the far edge of the bowl, where the trail ends, and looked across the bowl at the arch, and beyond to the

Crescent
moon rises
just before
sunrise.

"New Moon"
is invisible.

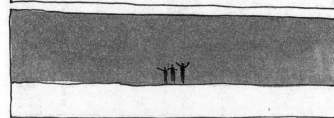

Crescent moon
sets shortly
after sunset.

Moon rises
about an hour
later each day;
about a week
later, a half-
moon ("First
Quarter" of
the lunar cycle)
is overhead at
sunset.

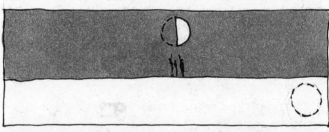

"Full Moon"
rises just
before sunset.

Another week
later, a half
moon is
overhead at
sunrise ("Last
Quarter").

Twisted Arch (*left*) forms the spotlight for Delicate Arch (*right*); the funnel-shaped bowl between them cannot be seen in this photograph from across the valley.

distant mountains. The shadows were lengthening. The sun was behind me in the western sky, heading northwest, and the shadow line was creeping up the bowl toward Delicate Arch.

Down at the bottom of the bowl, I noticed a spot of light in the midst of the shadow. Soon it had moved, angling up the bowl. And I realized that there must be a window in the rock somewhere behind me.

I picked my way carefully along the edge of the bowl to the south and, sure enough, there was a large opening in the rock, big enough for a few people to stand in. As I stood there, I could see the diffuse shadow that I created in the midst of the spotlight on the other side of the bowl below Delicate Arch.

The bowl, and Delicate Arch, and the distant mountains were all very dramatic even without the spotlight. The bowl is almost a natural amphitheater, its rim below the arch a natural stage, visible both for people sitting around the bowl and for any viewers on the other side of the little valley where the end-of-the-road viewpoint now is. And here we had a spotlight, angling up toward the stage as the sun set in the northwest sky.

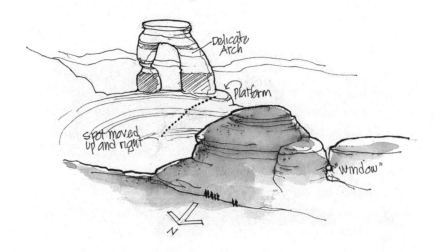

The elevated pedestal at the foot of Delicate Arch had plenty of room for someone to stand, a natural speaker's platform in the midst of all this natural seating for the multitudes. If the ancient Greeks had such a setting, they wouldn't have needed to build that amphitheater at Delphi. While Delphi may have steam-emitting springs on occasion, it lacks a built-in spotlight.

Delicate Arch's natural spotlight is not adjustable, however, being dependent on the sun's path through the sky. Though, I suppose, if a half-dozen people stood in the window, they could turn the spotlight on and off via kneeling and standing up (inadvertently casting a shadow on the spotlit priest might have had more severe consequences than mere shouts of "Sit down!"). I looked back through the window in the rock and saw a cliff in the west that would block the sunlight from reaching the window except when the sun was well into the northwestern sky. This only occurs near the summer solstice, in the half-hour before sunset. So that spotlight doesn't exist most of the year.

Fortunately, I was there only a few days after the summer solstice, and thus saw the shadows and the spotlight going as far southeast as they'd ever go. And the spotlight was angling up the bowl toward the speaker's platform. Weeks later, it would surely angle up to the middle of the pillar, not the end of the arch.

I snapped one picture after another, wondering whether the spotlight would wink out before ever reaching the little platform (which would ruin the best part of my theatrical theory). But about the time that the shadow line was approaching the top of Delicate Arch, the spotlight reached the platform. Someone standing there would have been bathed in a red-orange light (if I'd been thinking, I would have asked one of the other hikers to run around the rim and stand there). And then the reddish light would creep up the person, finally illuminating only the headdress. Then it would dim out as the sun set.

A climactic performance, just for me and a few other hikers. Would the prehistoric Indians have come in greater numbers? The Paleo-Indians were hunter-gatherers (not tied down all summer by hauling water to the plants if the thunderstorms dumped their rain in the wrong place) and hunter-gatherers have an important reason to hold big meetings. Each band was a closely interrelated group of perhaps 25 people. Incest prohibitions being what they are, prospective spouses came from another band.

Anthropologists have calculated that it takes a pool of at least 500 people (in other words, a *tribe* of 20 *bands*) for the unmarried to find more than one unmarried person of suitable age and opposite sex. So hunter-gatherers who wanted some choice in this important matter had a real motivation to get together regularly, even if they couldn't live together at that density for very long, food on the hoof being scattered the way it is. My guess is that Delicate Arch's spotlight was used by the chief shaman of a preagricultural tribe, that this is one place where they held their summer meeting—and that the transient nature of the spotlight gave them a reason to meet near the summer solstice.

46

IN THE OLD WORLD, THE STONE AGE SITES HAVE USU-
ally been built upon, repeatedly. What's worse, old materials
have been reused, confusing the archaeologist. And even
when the archaeologist finds a late neolithic construction,
such as Stonehenge or Avebury, relatively intact, one knows
little about the cultural traditions of the people who built it.
In the New World, you can find undisturbed sites. Even
better, there are Native Americans whose cultural traditions
have descended from Stone Age peoples, providing a glimpse
of the culture of the ancient builders.

The Pueblo Indians of the American Southwest are a
case in point. Their distant ancestors are among the Paleo-
Indians who crossed over from Asia to the Americas perhaps
15,000 years ago and subsequently followed the ice-free corridor east of the Rockies when it opened about 12,000 years
ago, allowing passage from Alaska to the mid-latitudes of
North America. About 2,300 years ago, some of the bands in
the desert southwest began to settle down to agriculture—
which is when one starts referring to them as "Anasazi"
rather than "Paleo-Indian." They may have acquired corn
(maize) and squash from the natives farther south, who were
the first to domesticate corn. These two staples for their diet
enabled their population to double and redouble over what
mere hunting and gathering would support.

The rains are fickle in this country, which is largely
mountainous desert, and so the Anasazi continued to get a
lot of their calories from nuts, cactus, rabbits, and bighorn
sheep. They'd have gotten into dietary troubles if they
hadn't supplemented with such hunter-gatherer items, since
corn and squash alone aren't a nutritionally balanced mini-
mal diet. When beans were later added, the three crops
would have made them largely independent of the wildlife
and nuts, but I suspect they treasured their traditional foods
and continued to seek them out—at least, on the occasions
when they weren't trapped, hauling water to their crops.
The occasions when they had the leisure to forage must

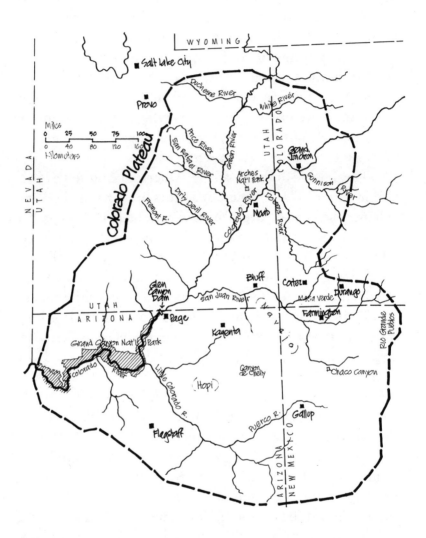

have been a pleasure, as some people today feel for "going shopping."

The Pueblo peoples are largely descendants of the Anasazi who took refuge in those Pueblo settings at the time of the great droughts between A.D. 1130 and about 1300. So the word "Anasazi" refers to a culture that existed from 2,300 years ago up until a substantial isolation and mixing with adjacent tribes (such as the Sinagua) took place about 700 years ago; its last phase produced the cliff-dwellings at places such as Mesa Verde. "Pueblo" refers to the living descendants of the Anasazi, who now prefer to live atop mesas and farm nearby. The remaining Pueblo Indian tribes are the Hopi, the Zuni, and several dozen smaller Rio Grande Pueblos (the latter tribes were largely Christianized by the industrious Spanish priests who came to New Mexico with the Spanish governor).

The Pueblos have, of course, likely undergone their own changes in the last 700 years, particularly as a consequence of the European culture that invaded the region with the Spanish Entrada of 1540, with more rapid changes occurring as settlers moved west in the nineteenth and twentieth centuries. "Historic Pueblo" tends to refer to the Pueblo culture in the period 1880-1895, when a series of anthropologists and diarists (often Protestant missionaries) recorded much about the Pueblos, at least those aspects that the Indians would show them and discuss.

The previous three centuries of presumably literate and curious Catholic clerics did not produce such a literature; this lack is likely a consequence of the intellectual intimidation of the Spanish Inquisition (initiated in the thirteenth century, the Inquisition was not finally suppressed until 1834). Since the Hopi, living in northern Arizona on high mesas about 100 kilometers east of the Grand Canyon, had been least affected by the Spanish priests working out of Santa Fe, New Mexico, the late-nineteenth-century Hopi culture is often assumed to be the closest to the original Anasazi culture, to the elements of the hunter-gatherer culture that preceded agriculture. However, the Hopi are traditionally secretive about ritual matters; for all we know, the essence of their ritual practice went unrecorded.

Still, whatever the limitations, one thus achieves a rare glimpse of the word-of-mouth culture of a temperate-zone Stone Age people. There are no such survivors of the European and Middle Eastern Stone Ages—for those long-gone cultures, one has only "hard evidence," the stone tools and broken pottery that have survived better than the wooden spears, sandals, carrying bags, and verbal culture. For the Anasazi, one even has pictographs and all sorts of soft evidence in the form of wood tools and intact necklaces. Despite the problems of inference back across several transitions, Anasazi archaeology and Pueblo ethnography give the archaeologist a lot to go on.

The pre-Columbian Americas in general, when compared to the Old World, give a unique view of another way to develop a high civilization than those followed by the peoples of the Fertile Crescent. Though more advanced than the Old World in certain areas (the Mayans were using the number zero well before the Old World; the Paleo-Indians domesticated corn, etc.), the lack of metal tools prevented the American cultures from straying very far away from the essentials. We marvel at their road systems (even though they lacked both wheeled vehicles and horses), at their extensive cultivation without the plow. And their art.

WHILE ANASAZI ROCK ART IS SOMETIMES FOUND OUT in the open, exposed to the weather, what remains is usually found protected under an overhang of some sort. There, the sun doesn't heat up (and expand) the surface rock every day, eventually causing it to soften and flake off. Permanent shadows help posterity, whether the rock art is painted (pictographs) or pecked into the rock surface (petroglyphs).

The Anasazi lived in a land of long, temporary shadows. Canyon country. Some of those moving shadows slowly sweep across rock art. Much has been written about the potential astronomical significance of the art-shadowline combination. Fajada Butte is perhaps the best known of the examples. High up one side of this freestanding butte, at the southern entrance to Chaco Canyon in New Mexico, are some fallen slabs of rock. If you crawl beneath them, you can see the midday shadows, narrowed to leave only a slit of light, move slowly across a spiral pecked into an underlying rock: the Sun Dagger, as the moving slit has been named.

It is said to mark the summer solstice—but one sees about the same thing for weeks. So far as I know, there is nothing that happens at Fajada which uniquely marks the exact day of the solstice. There is a lot of Anasazi rock art scattered around the Southwest that is specially shadowed near the solstices, so the illuminated spiral on the side of Fajada Butte probably was intended to celebrate the summer solstice. But it doesn't *mark* it, in the sense of specifying the day of turnaround. Watching the position of sunrise on the horizon would have worked better than the Sun Dagger.

More interesting are rock art depictions of the Crab Nebula supernova of A.D. 1054, the best of which is located at the other end of Chaco Canyon. There is little doubt that the Anasazi paid a lot of attention to the skies, especially at the solstices. So did they build a Stonehenge?

4

||||||||||||||||

Top-down and Bottom-up Views from the Grand Canyon

The sky broke like an egg into full sunset and the water caught fire.

PAMELA HANSFORD JOHNSON, *1981*

On the coast of Greece south of Athens are many places to see a beautiful sunset, shining across the sea. At the end of the peninsula, you also can see an unusual combination: As the full moon rises over the Aegean, the sun sets simultaneously in the gulf leading to Piraeus. The silvery shining waters lead from the eastern horizon toward you, and the rosy shining waters connect you to the western horizon. It feels a very privileged spot, as if something special is going on—and you are in the center of it.

I think that this rising and setting might have impressed the ancient Greeks, too, because the view is best at the Temple of Poseidon, built about the same time as the Parthenon in the middle of the fifth century B.C., and perched on a rocky "land's end" promontory jutting out into the sea like a giant breakwater. As the temple's elongated shadows reach out toward the moon, the red-tinted Doric columns create a frame, making the moon appear enormous. Soon the sun has set and the moon has risen higher in the sky, but for a few minutes the convergence of shining streaks produces a spectacle—perhaps not on the order of an eclipse, but ranking up there with, say, the view from Delphi.

Sunset shadows at the Temple of Poseidon.

WE HUMANS ARE OFTEN students of the sunset and, in the American Southwest, the remaining Native Americans often practice the nightly ritual of watching the sunset. They gather outside the doors to their dwellings, or climb up on the roof to watch the end of another day. I had to do without the roof when I watched a sunset over the Grand Canyon from the North Rim's Cape Royal, but Indians lived there about a thousand years ago so I was likely reenacting the local tradition. And I watched sunset on the night of the full moon, remembering that experience in Greece.

The thunderstorms of the afternoon had disappeared. I got soaked twice during the day along the North Rim. In most places in the American Southwest, you can see little rain squalls coming, just by looking around the horizon in the direction from which the wind is blowing. But on the canyon rim, at nearly 2,400 meters' (7,900 feet) elevation, you have to look down instead. Squalls rise up out of the depths of the Grand Canyon, something like an eruption from a boiling cauldron that the witches forgot to stir.

All of that well-heated air from summer sunshine in the canyon rises as updrafts—and runs into the moist air flowing north from the Gulf of Mexico during the monsoon season. A common result is a little turbulence that degenerates into patchy lightning and thunder. With the cooling of evening, the clouds often disappear, making possible a clear view of the western horizon.

Walhalla Plateau is a peninsula-in-the-sky at the southeastern corner of the canyon's North Rim. Cape Royal juts,

Sounion promontory and the Temple of Poseidon with sunset in the southwest.

promontory-like, south into the Canyon from the plateau, just as the temple's site juts into the Aegean from the tip of the Greek peninsula. You have to imagine the Grand Canyon full of water to complete the analogy. The southern tip of Cape Royal is open and flat, except for the sagebrush that dominates the landscape. Scattered piñon pine and juniper trees border the mesa top; more rain falls where the storm clouds crest the rim, so that the sage represents a rain shadow of sorts.

Seen from Cape Royal, sunset occurs over the Hualapai Indian Reservation on Coconino Plateau to the west, almost 50 miles away. And the moonrise is often over the Hopi Indian Reservation, on another high plateau about the same distance to the east. Thanks to the distances involved, the horizon is almost as flat as that seen from the Temple of Poseidon—but no shining seas are currently available to accentuate the contrasts, to connect you directly with the sunset or moonrise. Those yawning gaps are instead filled with warm colors and elaborate rock formations that cast long shadows.

Angel's Window is among the many thin ridgelines of

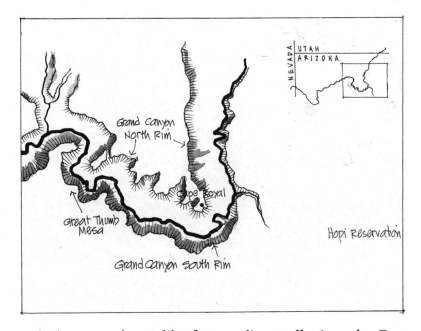

rock that extend out, like freestanding walls, into the Canyon for a short distance from Cape Royal, before abruptly terminating in a cliff. They are miniature peninsulas on the fringe of the big one, shaped like vertical fins and possessing some sage and pine atop their cracks and crevasses. A large chunk of limestone fell out of one of those thin walls but, surprisingly, without collapsing the top of the ridge. And so a "window" in the rock was created. I remember looking up from the Colorado River, on one of my float trips through the bottom of the Grand Canyon, and seeing the large triangular opening in the cliff face, blue sky showing through it. Up at Cape Royal, tourists walk atop the window and look down. Or stand back on the plateau to the west and see the Colorado River framed by the window.

Might this window function as a spotlight, like the one west of Delicate Arch? No, I reluctantly concluded. Only as it is setting can the sun be seen through the window—but it requires that the viewer be in the bottom of the Grand Canyon, standing in the right place. And the viewer would not be able to see any sign of a "spotlight" on the ground nearby. The "spot" created by the setting sun shining through the window is too diffuse to be detected, because the many miles between the window and the relevant areas of canyon bottom serve to smear out the shadow edges beyond recognition.

And it was such a good idea; I could have used a second example of the Delicate Arch drama.

Spotlights like the one at Delicate Arch are, of course, merely circular shadows. The direction of a shadow is a matter of the time of day and the time of year; the combination of sunset and summer solstice made that opening opposite Delicate Arch frame a shadow on the pedestal of Delicate Arch. While solstice shadows and sightlines are the usual preoccupation of archaeoastronomers, what about shadows and sights when an eclipse is due? Eclipses do not favor certain points of the compass (they can occur with the sunset anywhere between southwest and northwest), so no sightline is likely to be special to eclipses. But might sunset shadows point toward moonrise on special occasions?

Hmm. Does your own shadow reach out and "touch" the rising moon just prior to an eclipse? When that idea first occurred to me, I remember speaking firmly to myself, something to the effect that I was getting a little too theatrical in my scientific musings, that my brief career backstage running the lights for a high school ballet production must have gone to my head. But I didn't forget the notion of "touching the moon" with a shadow, connecting in a manner like those silvery streaks facilitated by rippling waters.

THE FULL MOON IS, OF COURSE (NOW THAT WE UN-derstand the geometry of eclipses), the only time at which lunar eclipses can occur. The moon has to be near the earth's shadow for an eclipse to threaten, and that also means that the moon will appear to be fully illuminated. The converse is not true; indeed, not only are the full moons of most months without eclipses, but the moon appears, arguably, to be full for a few nights each month (at least, my wife and I often argue about whether it is fully illuminated or not).

Which night might prehistoric people have celebrated as

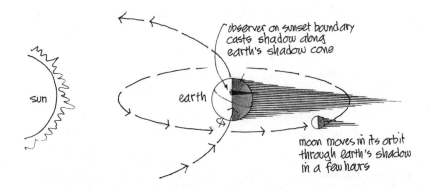

the "full moon," if fullness is so equivocal? My guess is that "full moon" (besides being called something else) was originally defined as the one evening of the month when the moon rises just before sunset—and so sits on the eastern horizon looking especially dramatic, colored by the sunset, with elongated shadows directing your attention toward it, and looming large (for some reason hidden inside our brain circuitry, the moon or sun sitting on the horizon looks a lot larger than when high in the sky).

The previous night, the moon rises an hour before sunset and seldom gains the coloring; it stands high in the sky, white and small at the time of sunset. The night after the full moon, the sunset colors are often gone by the time that the moon (still looking quite full) appears on the eastern horizon. So on one night of this sequence, the moonrise is much more noticeable than usual. Before I could correct myself for relying on drama again, I remembered (modern geometry speaking again) that moonrise-just-before-sunset was an essential setup for a lunar eclipse later that evening. That definition of "fullness" would, it so happens, be one that facilitated eclipse forecasting.

But, since lunar eclipses don't occur every month, which month's full moon portends an eclipse? How do we sort this out? Or rather, how might a prehistoric people have sorted it out?

MOONRISE AND SUNSET CAME AND WENT; THE Grand Canyon dimmed to moonlight levels of illumination. The combination moonrise and sunset was a wonderful view; those canyon colors are quite distracting but I did manage to watch my shadow grow longer and longer. It pointed in the general direction of the moon, but I could tell that my shadow wasn't going to come close to the moon.

You need a good unobstructed path to play this game. The shadow becomes dimmer at the same time as it grows longer, and it slowly changes direction, sweeping slightly to the south. That's because the sun is angling toward the northwest as it sets, sweeping those long shadows toward the southeast.

What's the relationship, if any, between shadow directions and lunar eclipses? The North Rim has no handy library with canons of eclipses and angles of moonrise and sunset to consult. But the little computer in my daypack had the programs for calculating the angles. Though I would like an excuse to visit the Grand Canyon at each full moon for the next year, I really could run time forward and backward in the computer, simulating what I'd see each month.

BY THE MIDDLE OF THE NEXT DAY (NO ECLIPSE OCcurred, by the way), several answers had become clear. If the moon is well into the sky by the time of sunset, an eclipse is impossible (even if the shadows point directly toward the moon); even ten minutes between moonrise and sunset are enough to rule out an eclipse in most cases. Eclipses are also impossible when the sun sets before moonrise (assuming horizons without much elevation).

Hmm. Before time measurement, they probably used the *height* of the moon at sunset as a simple way of ruling out eclipses. If the moon is more than a few diameters off the eastern horizon when the sun is sitting on the western horizon, a lunar eclipse is unlikely.

It's Method #4 ("High Moon Is Safe"). If you have a

prediction scheme such as counting by sixes, this moon height observation at sunset will provide a way of *ruling out* an otherwise predicted lunar eclipse, rather like you might look out the window in the morning to check the validity of yesterday's weather forecast. You'll be able to rest assured that the prayers will be answered, and perhaps gain some credibility at the expense of your competitors in the prophet business, who are raising the usual alarms on the sixth month following an eclipse. You can just look calm and assured, going around telling people that you *know* an eclipse won't happen, whatever those other prophets claim, because you have a better pipeline to the Almighty.

The method seems simple enough to have been discovered in prehistoric times. I certainly wasn't the first to discover it in modern times as it is mentioned in passing in the very book that, a quarter-century earlier, originally stimulated my interest in eclipse forecasting:

> It seems most probable that the Stonehengers noted and made use of that moonrise-sunset time relation to predict eclipses. Compared to the task of determining the eclipse year and month by use of the Aubrey Holes and rise-set directions, the foretelling of the night and the hour of the event by observation of the difference in time between moonrise and sunset would have been easy.
>
> GERALD S. HAWKINS, *Stonehenge Decoded*, 1965

BACK TO SHADOWS, HOWEVER. THE SECOND INSIGHT from all of my number crunching: When the sunset shadows are within a diameter or so to the *left* of the rising moon on the horizon, a lunar eclipse is particularly likely.

For about four centuries, we have known that the earth casts a cone-shaped shadow, the umbra, in the same direction as the observer's shadow. This shadow cone rises unseen in the east, just as the sun sets in the west. Indeed, the observer's sunset shadow is sometimes a tiny part of the cone, a little dim bump on the right side of it.

An eclipse occurs when the moon's eastward orbital motion during the night carries it left, into that conical shadow (well, at least as seen by observers in the Northern Hemisphere). But the prescientific observer need not know that in order to associate "touching the moon with your shadow" with an eclipse. So *sunset shadows pointing near the rising moon*  *(within a few diameters to its left)* constitute Method #5 ("Touching the Moonrise") for eclipse forecasting, once again "entry-level" in its simplicity for the prospective prophet.

The method doesn't always work (the moon's path sometimes goes just above or below the umbra) but every eclipse will have been preceded by such a coincidence. The moon has to be close to the cone-shaped shadow at sunset to stand any chance of moving into the shadow within the next several hours. The scheme, particularly effective for those lunar eclipses that happen in the several hours after sunset, serves to warn of those lunar eclipses that happen when many people are still awake, rather like the pinhole methods give an hour's warning of a total solar eclipse.

Wider separations between moonrise and sunset shadows may also be associated with eclipses later in the night, but the judgment becomes complicated, making it hard to improve on the probability suggested by the counting-by-sixes prediction. With Method #1 ("Clenched Fist Counting"), you may know that there is a substantial probability of an eclipse; with Method #4 ("High Moon Is Safe") or #5 ("Touching the Moonrise"), you may be able to rule it out (as in the case of sunset before moonrise) or to raise the alarm (when the last shadows point at a just-rising moon, as must have been the case in Jamaica in 1504).

TALL PEOPLE MIGHT HAVE an advantage at playing this sunset shadow game. Shorter people might want to wear tall headgear of some sort, or just use a dead tree that is standing upright like a utility pole; you stand with your back to it and sight along its shadow at the rising moon. Ancient observers might have even climbed to the top of a post or column, to better observe the shadow's direction.

Now that's what they might have been doing at the Temple of Poseidon—using the sunset shadows of those Doric columns, stretching out across the marble floor and meeting the shining streak of sea, leading from the moonrise.

The observer stands at the base of a western column, sights along the column's shadow leading across the floor to the eastern columns, and judges if it lines up with the streak of silvery sea arriving from the rising moon—or if it produces too much of a dogleg-like angle. Checking that sort of alignment, seeing if two straight-line segments convincingly merge into one straight line, is even easier than tracing one's shadow outward toward the moon. Evolving a criterion for how–close–is–close can be aided by the columns themselves, such as requiring that the moonrise be within a column's width of the sunset shadow.

So is the Temple of Poseidon an architectural solution to eclipse forecasting: tall columns, built in a good locale (long views both east and west)? Suppose that the tall stones of Stonehenge were for the same purpose, the priests sighting down a stone's shadow to see if the moon rose at its very end?

WITHOUT AN EASTERN COASTLINE, YOU CAN'T USE the silvery streak. Even if you have the requisite eastern view, shadows can be hard to judge, particularly final alignments:

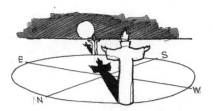

How dim is dim enough? And shadows can be diffused by all the humidity that dims ocean sunsets (and makes moonrises ghostly).

You can often solve shadow alignment problems by looking directly at the setting sun, getting your line of sight from the sun itself rather than a shadow. Trouble is, I mused, how can you do that if you also have to look at the rising moon? Yes, I know that you can turn around, but how do you know that you've turned exactly half a circle, short of using a modern surveying instrument?

The low-tech solution (indeed, no-tech—just naked eye and found objects) is to use *two* observers, standing some distance apart from one another. The Eastern Observer stands still while the Western Observer walks around until the rising moon is located just behind the Eastern—and then remains rooted to the spot, while the Eastern Observer (continuing to stand still) sights past the Western toward the setting sun. If the setting sun is indeed behind the Western Observer, then the observers must be on the line from sun to moon, with no dogleg angle.

The moon "touching" the Eastern Observer's outstretched arm could also qualify—and thus provide a measure of the offset between moonrise and sunset shadow line (given some standard number of paces between the two observers). Like the within-a-column's-width criterion for matching up a Doric column's shadow with the moonrise, this would allow a tradition to develop concerning when to raise the alarm and when to let an ambiguous situation pass. It would give a clear yes-or-no answer (which always helps to reduce arguments!).

Now it seems unlikely that prescientific peoples would have formulated the rule as a "straight line" relationship. They'd have personified things, if folk culture is any clue. They might have called Eastern Observer the "Sun Priest"

because he watched the sunset, called the Western Observer the "Moon Priest" (or some such). They would have watched for those occasions when the sun "touched" the Moon Priest in the same manner as the rising moon had "touched" the Sun Priest. Symmetry, no less.

WERE THESE SIMPLE SCHEMES ever used? By the time writing was invented, fancier eclipse-prediction schemes may have overlain the simple ones, caused them to be discarded as obsolete. I do know of one priestly practice among the Pueblo Indians that might correspond to my Two Priests method, though we should be cautious in interpreting rituals whose purposes may have drifted away from their original ones.

The Anasazi have living descendants who think that eclipses are bad luck, cause the deaths of children, and cause crops to fail. I wouldn't be surprised if the Anasazi were similarly apprehensive about eclipses. Mentions of eclipses in the Pueblo literature are rare, but fear might have made eclipses taboo subjects for conversation, unlikely to be mentioned to an anthropologist or missionary. But there is a revealing story about a practice of two priests, reported by the anthropologist Florence H. Ellis from a pueblo in New Mexico, that strongly suggests (at least, to me) a procedure for eclipse prediction:

Each evening, they note the place of sunset and moonrise: "The moon is believed to travel between the north and the south just as the sun does but at opposite seasons so that their paths cross at one point. The matter of

66

prime importance to these calendar priests . . . is to *observe Sun and full Moon exactly when they most closely approach each other* [emphasis added], a problem duplicating that of the Zuni. . . . "

Yet for the *full* moon to be in the same place as the sun is patently impossible, so what's going on here?

With a somewhat different metaphorical translation allowing some ambiguity between the setting sun and a "sun priest" (perhaps the same word was used for both?), this might correspond to my Two Priests method: the full Moon approaching the Sun [Priest] and the Sun approaching the Moon [Priest]. Ambiguity has its uses, even for eclipse prediction.

A certain duality between sun and moon, between day and night, between winter and summer is deeply embedded in Pueblo concepts. They conceive of an underworld that is a half-year in advance of the real world—except that, in the underworld, the moon may take the sun's role. You can see where they might get the idea of the full moon playing the sun's role in the underworld: In the winter, when the sun makes a low arc across the southern sky during the day, the full moon is making a high arc that same night— indeed, tracing a path similar to that taken by the sun in the summertime. And in the summer when the sun is high in the sky, the full moon traces a low arc like that of the winter sun. It would seem that an underworld notion might be helpful in evolving away from flat-earth models, toward schemes that, whatever their deficiencies, were handy for eclipse forecasting.

The Two Priests method is likely to be a refinement of a one-observer method—at least, I can imagine stumbling into the shadow-touching-the-moon scheme while I cannot imagine any two people discovering the choreography associated with this method, absent some predecessor methods. Still, either is a relatively simple method that makes no demands on geometrical understanding—it just requires that you have a reasonably flat horizon to the east *and* west, and develop some rituals for watching full moons at sunset. Particularly if used in combination with the clenched-fist forecast or a magic number scheme, the sun and moon lining up might have provided a reasonably accurate warning of an impending lunar eclipse.

BEFORE LEAVING CAPE ROYAL THE NEXT DAY, I FOUND an instructive view down—indeed, straight down. Unkar Creek is over a thousand meters below and, by the time that the creek arrives at the Colorado River in the center of the Grand Canyon, the elevation difference is a vertical mile. With the aid of binoculars, you can see a short stretch of the Colorado River from Cape Royal, where Unkar Creek finishes up.

Down along Unkar Creek are the thousand-year-old ruins of the winter homes of the Anasazi, probably the same families as lived up here on the Walhalla Plateau during the summer. They went south for the winter, down to where it is warmer. When the North Rim is buried in massive snowdrifts, the bottom of the Grand Canyon is merely a little cool and rainy.

Such is the difference that elevation makes. The bottom of the Grand Canyon was a good place to shelter from the winter weather, with nuts to gather and game to hunt. At Unkar Delta near the river, the major farming area for the Unkar Creek people, archaeologists find lots of bones from bighorn sheep, deer, and rabbits. Even in the days before rainfall improved enough to allow farming, the local tribes probably did a lot of wintertime hunting and gathering in the bottom of the canyon.

THE BOTTOM-UP VIEW IS EVEN MORE IMPRESSIVE; YOU wouldn't want to practice any of the eclipse methods associated with sunset shadows touching the moonrise, since the horizons are greatly elevated. Traveling down the Colorado River into the bottom of the Grand Canyon is like having a

range of mountains grow up around you; with each passing day, they get taller.

Downstream of the confluence with the Little Colorado River at Mile 61 below Lee's Ferry (the usual place where river trips begin), the Colorado River's narrow gorge opens out for about ten miles, takes a U-turn around Unkar Delta at Mile 73, whereupon the canyon walls close back in. The Anasazi farmed all along the stretch of more open river bottom, irrigating their maize, squash, and beans with water hauled from the river.

On my third trip down the river, I saw a particularly long and spectacular lunar eclipse just after visiting Unkar Delta, in fact. That night, I was across the river, atop a minor hilltop with a good view of the expanse of Grand Canyon. The hilltop was distinguished by a minor ruin. Though it was only four walls made of piles of flat stones, the Cardenas Hilltop Ruin was something of an enigma. It seemed too far away from the agricultural sites (and drinking water) to be a habitation. Though a nice site for a guardpost because of its long views, it was really too large. Given the eclipse in progress, I couldn't help contrasting it to Stonehenge, wondering if it was built there with some astronomical purpose in mind.

Tracking the sunrise's movements along the horizon, from its southeast extreme of winter to its northeast extreme of summer, was the first possibly prehistoric scheme that occurred to me while waiting for totality to end. Compared to the featureless horizon of Salisbury Plain, the bottom-up view from the depths of the Grand Canyon is far better for tracking the seasons. The hilltop ruin would have been just the place for the Unkar Delta people to "keep a calendar" for planting time. Each morning in winter and spring, the sun rises farther north—until, at the summer solstice, the sunrise turns around and heads south again. One of those notches in the South Rim could be the Unkar Delta people's reminder: When the sun finally rises on that notch, it's time to plant corn.

If you can't have a nice level sea horizon, better to have a jagged one, I thought. Mountain peaks and the notches between them function nicely as markers—so long as you maintain a customary point of observation, such as your front doorway. Or a favorite hilltop.

I remember examining the eastern skyline in the moonlight. The Palisades of the Desert is an expanse of canyon rim with a vertically scalloped cliff. A regular series of promontories stick out, like folds of a hanging curtain—or, I suppose, the Doric columns on a Greek temple. All through the spring and summer, the sunrise would move along those notches. The Anasazi could have easily given the notches names, just as we name the months.

And so I counted the number of notches in the skyline as best I could in the fading moonlight. Between the approximately due-east sunrise of the spring equinox and the north-easterly sunrise at the summer solstice, the sunrise position would shift sideways past at least a dozen easily identifiable markers. A dozen in three months means about one every week, on the average. That's a pretty detailed calendar for agriculture, as you don't need to count down the days.

When I scanned the southeast horizon where the sunrise should be in autumn and winter, I found that I couldn't see the South Rim because a large butte inside the canyon obscured my view from the hilltop ruin. The butte wasn't more than a few kilometers away and rose up rather high in the sky. That means that sunrise in the winter must have been pretty late. Might there be a special notch for the winter solstice sunrise, I mused, maybe in that nice V-shaped notch?

The winter solstice is the focal point of the Hopi's high religious festivals, I remembered. For a week or so, the position of sunrise changes so imperceptibly that people speak of the sun "standing still." Then it begins rising somewhat farther north each day. From Cardenas Hilltop Ruin, I estimated, it would reach the Palisades by spring and then continue through that series of notches during the springtime. The Hopi are known for spreading their bets by planting at different times in different places, so perhaps each one of those Palisade notches marked a time to plant. I wondered briefly about a big promontory with a pinnacle projecting from it, Comanche Point—what date might it correspond to?

From where the Hopi tribe now lives just to the east of the Grand Canyon, they use the position of sunset over mountain peaks to mark the winter solstice, the time for religious festivals and planting corn, etc. The Indians who lived in Puget Sound could have easily done the same thing, what with the sunrise skipping from one mountaintop to another in the Cascades as the weeks go by—and the sunset traversing the peaks of the Olympics as well (it's between the twin peaks of The Brothers at the equinoxes, at least from Seattle). If you've named each peak and notch, as seen from

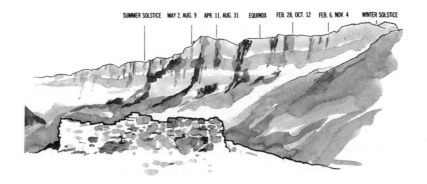

some customary viewpoint, you can often infer "today's date" to within a day or two of what a modern calendar would tell you (except near the solstices).

After my river trip, I constructed a horizon calendar for the view from the hilltop ruin—not by spending a year there watching the sunrise, but with the aid of photographs, a topographic map, and the computer. Comanche Point turns out to be at the end of April.

The diligent observer experiences great difficulty at the extreme positions because the position of sunrise changes so slowly from day to day. If you want to celebrate the turn-around, and your method can't spot the reversal until a few days after it actually starts, then your winter solstice celebrations will occur—Christmas Day!

STONEHENGE SIGHTLINES MARK THE SAME SUN AND moon extremes, and for both eastern and western horizons. And I suppose that some of the other stones at Stonehenge and Avebury could mark other significant dates. But given how well a jagged horizon works for keeping a versatile seasonal calendar (and many river valleys, bounded by eroding bluffs, will work almost as well as the Grand Canyon), why build Stonehenge and Avebury where the horizons are instead largely featureless? If you only measure the solar extremes, where day-to-day change is so slow that the "reading errors" must have been considerable, you can easily miss the day of winter solstice by a week or more (especially with

the kind of winter weather experienced in England) and have
your calendar off by a week for the next six months. Using
solstice-only sightlines is a terrible way to run a calendar, so
bad that you'd think that only a few examples would be
found, remnants of a failed experiment.

That leads me to suppose that the megalithic monuments emphasizing solstice sightlines were for some purpose
other than an agricultural calendar—a purpose that, inciden-
tally, needed such solstice sightlines. Eclipse prediction? I've
already discovered (likely rediscovered) simpler methods of
predicting most lunar eclipses, and warning of solar eclipses.
Nothing like Stonehenge is really required, neither its solstice
alignments nor its 56-hole circle.

Yet solstice alignments are clearly the most common
feature of the hundreds of archaeoastronomy sites around the
world, even if it is absurd to run a calendar keyed to them.
What made them so popular? Religion might have spread
solstice constructions around from one community to another, despite marginal practical utility. But in both Old
World and New World? Surely we're missing something
here.

Call the solstice alignments *Exhibit B* for the skeptical
defense (whose chorus chants, "But you haven't explained
the archaeology yet!"). And I haven't had any luck explaining
Exhibit A either (the artificially smoothed horizons, such as
the elevated bank at Avebury). Whatever were they using
them for?

> When the people see [an eclipse], they then raise a tu-
> mult. And a great fear taketh them, and then the women
> weep aloud. And the men cry out, striking their mouths
> with their hands . . . and they said, "If the sun becometh
> completely eclipsed never more will he give light; eter-
> nal darkness will fall, and the demons will come down.
> They will come to eat us!"
>
> from a sixteenth-century Aztec history text

5

||||||||||||||

The View from an Anasazi Cave

To me the most interesting thing about man is that he is an animal who practices art and science and, in every known society, practices both together.

JACOB BRONOWSKI, 1967

Caves play a large role in our concepts of the prehistoric past. We talk of "cavemen" or, if we like fancy words with which to slander an opponent, "troglodytes" (Latin for cave dwellers). The cave-dwelling cultures span quite a spectrum, even as one goes north up the Dordogne River valley in France. Downstream is Cro-Magnon (the site for which the people were named), not even a proper cave but more of an overhang, a "rock shelter" that isn't really enclosed against the cold winds but at least stays dry in a rainstorm. Such sheltered areas are often found with fire pits and lots of charred animal bones—but not much in the way of ruins, the remains of dwellings that were regularly inhabited. One supposes that Cro-Magnon provided seasonal shelter for a wandering band of hunter-gatherers in the last ice age.

Archaeologists love rock shelters; the floors tend to build up higher and higher over the years, what with pieces of the overhang collapsing and windblown soil collecting and compacting. Digging down, the archaeologist finds a series of layers that can be dated (usually using radiocarbon methods on the organic matter). In these layers are cultural artefacts such as stone tools.

This Anasazi deer figure is pecked into the cliff wall and outlined with a white pigment. Note the spear and its lack of perspective.

Stick figures (*above*) are not common in Anasazi rock art. More typical are the triangular-shaped torsos with short legs and arms (*below*).

Upstream from Cro-Magnon is Lascaux, a subterranean cavern of considerable extent containing some of the finest of Ice Age art. Many European caves have carvings and drawings of objects, though not on a wide range of subject matter. The subject always seems to be a topic of considerable interest to the adolescent boys—who are, after all, the most likely cave explorers. Typical subjects are nubile women, virile hunters, and challenging game animals—but not nursing babies or young children at play. One suspects that the intended audience was also exclusively young and male. Yet despite this impoverishment in subject matter, such caverns as Lascaux in the Dordogne, Niaux in the Pyrenees, and Altamira on the north coast of Spain nonetheless contain serious art by most standards, with a careful use of color and texture (such as using the cracks and ridges in the rock face to lend dimensionality to the representation of a suitably situated bison).

In the American Southwest, rock shelters often have Anasazi ruins under the overhang. The Indians built houses and ceremonial rooms (kivas) there and farmed nearby plots to supplement their hunting-and-gathering diet. The same "cliff dwellings" often have an Anasazi art gallery nearby. To see them may require hiking for a few days, as is the case with one of my favorite places, Anasazi Valley.

Green "monster" (*left*) with human face threatens Giacometti-like slender figures (in white at *right*) in this unusual scene from Anasazi rock art.

A GULLY THAT BECOMES A canyon is one way to describe Anasazi Valley. It cuts deeply into a high mesa, thanks to the rainfall running off some local mountains. The meandering stream cut deeper and deeper into the sandstone. After Anasazi Valley has twisted and turned dozens of times, the stream eventually reaches the even larger canyon carved by a river.

Anasazi Valley has the reputation for being the place that archaeologists go for their vacations. If you really want to soak up the atmosphere that the Anasazi lived and breathed, without the overlay of recreational vehicles and gift shops that has developed at the well-worn Anasazi sites such as Mesa Verde, you spend a week hiking down Anasazi Valley. Or even two weeks, if you want to go all the way down to the

Anasazi handprints are sometimes found by the dozens, in either a red or green pigment, and some are decorated. Quite a few handprints feature extra fingers, probably created by moving a finger to make a second impression. Note the two strays of paint (*left*) presumably blown from someone's mouth.

river and back. You cannot see even a part of it in an ordinary day hike. You've got to be serious about your Anasazi,

These twin spirals are made with mud, adhering to a smoke-blackened rock face forming the rear wall of a small kiva.

and willing to walk for a week, before you get to see this paradise.

I went down with Don Keller, an archaeologist at the Museum of Northern Arizona's research division. He's a specialist in the Anasazi, and has spent whole seasons digging in Anasazi Valley (and coping with the damage done by looters). Ken Theissen, a geologist, was also along and helped straighten out my confusions about the rock layers and the enormous forces that bent and twisted them.

After a day spent backpacking down a side canyon that had been transformed by grazing cattle, we were rewarded by a grand sight—Anasazi Valley itself. And this first view came complete with a cliff dwelling halfway up the far wall. Turkey Pen Ruin got its name from an unusual enclosure that the archaeologists uncovered, where the Anasazi had apparently penned up a turkey or two. They may well have valued birds for their feathers rather than their flesh. Parrots have also been found in Anasazi ruins such as Chaco Canyon's Pueblo Bonito, showing that the Anasazi traded with Central America. I suspect that turkey feathers were a poor man's substitute for those of the brightly colored parrots. The Pueblo people's prayer sticks, often left in shrines in the hillsides, are adorned with bird feathers.

Anasazi "Kokopeli" petroglyph with serpent petroglyph visible below. The hunchbacked flute player plays a role in the Pueblo legends.

Turkey Pen Ruin was built on several levels, as we discovered the next morning after breakfast. The floor of the canyon itself was used to build many rooms, nestled under the overhang provided by the alcove. It was surely where the people did most of their cooking, where the children played, where the turkey was kept. But a path leads up the sandstone to a set of steps cut into the rock, and the moderately agile can make it up to a long shelf inside the alcove, no more than one room deep, something like

"Tally Marks" are seldom vertical; these dozen marks ascend and are capped by a thirteenth mark.

the second balcony in an opera house. A kiva is near one end, and is so large that it completely blocks passage (and a modest sign requests that the visitor not climb atop the kiva).

The view from this ledge is beautiful but limited: Anasazi Valley twists and turns, thanks to the entrenched meanders, and one cannot see very far up or down the canyon. The peaceful green bottomlands, now thick with trees and scrubs, were likely cleared by the Anasazi for fields on which to grow corn.

It started to rain as we explored the ruin, but we were in no danger of getting wet; it would take hurricane-force winds to drive the rain far enough back under the overhang to reach the dwellings. Our campsite, however, was across the stream in a small clearing, and we remembered all of the sleeping bags left out to air. But several people were still in camp, and we saw them putting things away for the rest of us. I, as usual, had decided to leave my tent behind rather than carry the extra weight in my backpack, and I began to worry whether the rain might become a regular thing during the coming week. It was, after all, the summer monsoon season.

When I gingerly lowered myself back down the cliff to the sandy floor of the alcove, I saw that there are more pictographs than I first noticed. There is nothing like that kind of rock art at Mesa Verde (and if there were, they'd have to put up glass to shield it).

HIKING DOWN ANASAZI VALLEY REQUIRED CONSTANT stops, to look under the overhangs on each side of the widening valley. Many of the overhangs would make good rock shelters, but this isn't the Dordogne—Anasazi Valley has real amphitheaters in great numbers, good housing at essentially each meander. The overhangs are still a good place to shelter from the midday sun, and they had flat walls for the Anasazi artist—walls protected over the centuries from rainfall and sunshine.

All sorts of pictographs and petroglyphs are to be seen under overhangs. Some of the art depicts men on horseback, a clear giveaway that the Anasazi didn't draw it since North America lacked horses and humans together until the Spanish reintroduced the horse after 1540. Such art is likely Navajo, or even due to the Anglo cow herders of the last century. The themes of Anasazi art are not realistic: Their humanlike figures often involve distortion on a grand scale. Barrel chests tapering to narrower hips, with little feet and pinheads. Hand prints are the most realistic depiction, since they had a model to trace. And there are occasionally straight lines in a row, looking for all the world like tally marks. Their meaning is unknown, and I couldn't preferentially find groups of six or twelve. No clenched fists, either.

SPLIT-LEVEL RUIN IS HOUSED IN AN ENORMOUS AL-cove, looking south down Anasazi Valley. The stream wanders by, not far from the alcove, and the sandy floor between stream and alcove provided us with a lovely campsite. A light rain had started in the early morning light and I had spread my poncho over my sleeping bag and tried to get back to sleep.

The rain had gotten more and more serious, and I kept regretting the tent that I'd left behind. The rain dripped onto the ground cloth and drained under the sleeping bag. So while my top was dry, the moisture was wicking up from below.

Finally, I realized the obvious solution: Move from the campsite into the Anasazi alcove. The drip line was easy to see, and back of it the sandstone was totally dry. Not exactly level, but I'd given up on sleep by then. I spread the sleeping bag out on a rock to dry and started to explore the alcove in the new light of day.

The alcove housing Split-Level Ruin is a football field in width, and its depth considerable. As usual, there is a very high ledge that seems impossible to reach, yet it has evidence of grain storage structures. I'll bet that is where the Anasazi kept the seed corn, that essential supply for producing *next* year's harvest, to protect it in times of famine. At the east end is a collection of old timbers and the suggestion of an old structure, which I walked down to explore.

There wasn't much remaining of the ancient dwelling, except for the view they had from their doorway. Because the Anasazi picked alcoves that faced south, the view from their dwelling was always of the southern skyline, the source of winter warmth.

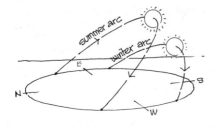

The view from inside an alcove is restricted, but in a lovely way. The cliffs across the canyon form an elevated horizon. The sky above your head is, of course, obscured by the overhang. Following the overhang down to the left, the alcove overhang and distant cliff horizon meet in a corner of sky. So you see a crescent of sky, pinched down to an acute corner in the southeast.

And the same thing happens to the right corner of sky: the overhang to the west comes down and meets another cliffy horizon in the southwest. When they were snug back inside the alcove, the Anasazi saw the world around them as a crescent of sky.

AS I LOOKED AT THE CRESCENT OF SKY ENDING IN the two acute corners, it dawned on me: Southeast and southwest were very important directions to the Anasazi. At pueblos such as Hopi and Zuni, they don't use our familiar north-east-south-west but rather the same solstice sightlines as Stonehenge. The cardinal directions to which they referred all others, just as we might make a construction such as "south-southeast," are

- the northeasterly direction of summer solstice sunrise (about *60°* from true north, in these latitudes; *90°* is east, *180°* is south, *270°* is west, *360°* is north again),
- the southeasterly direction of winter solstice sunrise (about *120°* hereabouts),
- the southwesterly direction of winter solstice sunset (*240°*), and
- the northwesterly direction of summer solstice sunset (*300°*).

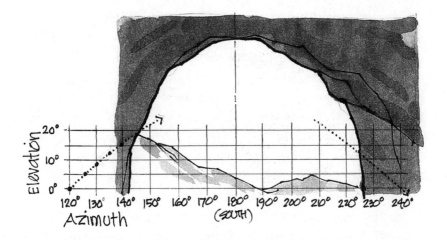

The view from an arbitrary rock shelter.

Were the crescent corners in two of the cardinal directions? There was only one way to find out, and it involved getting wet again. I ventured out into the rain and ran over to where my backpack was sheltering under its raincover. The side compartment had my pocket transit, which looks like a hefty pocket compass and functions as a combination of magnetic compass and elevation-measuring instrument. It's typically used by geologists for rough measurements when out hiking. I ran back into the dry alcove, the little instrument clutched close.

I climbed back up to the timbers and sat down to make the measurements on the crescent corners of skyline. I sighted to the right corner in the southwest. The bearing was about *215°* around from true north. Now I knew that winter solstice sunset is at about *240°* at these latitudes, but that's with a level horizon, and they'd have never seen the sun reach the level horizon because the high corner would have cut off their view while the sun was still high in the sky, probably an hour before sunset seen from the top walls of the canyon. One has to compensate for that elevated horizon.

Next I measured how high the corner was elevated from the horizontal, determined by a little bubble level inside the instrument. About 9°, which means that the sun wouldn't set

85

in the corner at all; it would be 20° high in the sky when reaching *215°*.

Then I tried the left corner of the crescent of sky seen from the timbers. It was elevated by only 18°, meaning that the solstice sunrise should occur in the southeast at about *140°* for my theory to be correct. And sure enough, the corner was about *140°*. So the left corner was where the Anasazi who lived here saw the sun rise on the shortest day of the year, the winter solstice.

One corner nearly works, but the other is way off—they wouldn't have seen the sun set in the right corner later that day. But obviously, the directions of the corners depend on where one stands within the alcove. Perhaps, I reasoned, if I moved over toward Split-Level Ruin itself, the southwest corner might come closer to the sun's path through the sky on the day of its southernmost journey. Maybe there is a "right place," where both crescent corners are cardinal directions.

And as I walked over toward the ruined kiva at Split-Level Ruin, I could see that the southwest corner was dipping lower and lower as more of the cliffs across the way came into view. Their intersection with the alcove overhang line became lower and lower, but my sightline was also swinging around farther to the west—where the sun is lower. Of course, the southeast corner of the crescent was also changing a little as I walked east.

I stood out in front of the ruined kiva, and measured the southeast corner first. It was now at *141°* and elevated 18.5°, right on the sun's path through the morning sky if my little instrument was correct. That suggested that a number of places in the alcove between the timber pile and the ruin probably had the winter solstice sunrise in the left crescent corner.

Then I measured the southwest corner of the crescent of sky: *228°* and elevated 8.0°, a few degrees below the sun's path. But somewhere close to the ruin, likely in front of it (so that the right corner moves back to *232°* and 8° high) where the slope is now eroded away, the sun should rise on the day of the winter solstice in one corner of the crescent and later set in the other corner of the crescent.

That is the favorite time of year in Pueblo ceremonial calendars. Maybe they built their kiva up and out to get to the right place, in the manner of rear decks on split-level residences of familiar suburbia?

Any south-facing alcove is going to have a view that is a crescent of sky with corners somewhere in the eastern and western skies. I suspect many alcoves aren't deep enough to get the corners to come out in the cardinal directions; Turkey Pen sure wasn't. But it worked at Split-Level Ruin's alcove. And it looked as if they'd built their kiva close to "the right spot."

Breakfast was anticlimactic.

GREEN MASK RUIN WAS OUR NEXT CAMPSITE, though not intentionally. We had intended to sleep on the opposite hillside, but it rained hard enough to make us regret the usual rule about camping close to ruins: the ruin was the only shelter in the area.

The original archaeologists had apparently faced this problem before us, and created a suitable campsite under the overhang but away from the ruins. It was just large enough to accommodate our party. And our leader was an archaeologist who knew the site quite well, and could keep us from doing harm. So I stayed dry that night after all.

The place was comfortable, as rock shelters go; the ruins are in an elevated portion around the corner and look down on the floor where we were. The light was poor, so we put off exploration until morning.

The evening was memorable. I had gone to sleep even before sunset, up on a slab of rock that angled toward the ceiling. I awoke several hours later after dark, strangely disoriented. I saw firelight and flickering shadows on the cave's ceiling, just as some Anasazi must have done, a thousand years earlier. Great distorted shadows moved across the ceiling as someone shifted position near the campfire. I heard an ethereal voice and a mandolin.

I can believe in an Anasazi with an ethereal voice, but I had trouble with the mandolin. The Anasazi, I believe that I can say with certainty, did not possess even a single mandolin. But Don Keller does and, having carried it atop his backpack, he was engaging in an archaeologist's evening entertainment in the resonant surroundings of a cliff dwelling. I lay there under the flickering ceiling and listened for a half hour before getting up and joining the group. Such are my experiences as a temporary troglodyte.

The next morning, we explored the ruins and looked up into a corner of the ceiling, well out of reach. There, all by itself, was the pictograph that gave the site its name. It depicted a green face mask, which was utterly unlike any of the Anasazi or Navajo art that we had been seeing. Don said that it is Basketmaker II in style, which in local archaeological usage tends to mean A.D. 200–400.

JAILHOUSE RUIN WAS UP ABOVE OUR FOURTH CAMP-site, nestled back in the cliff, and you can see where it got its name. There are bars in the windows of the ruin.

But "paleo-rebar ruin" might be a better description. Just as concrete walls these days are strengthened by creating a rough network of steel reinforcing bars ("rebar") before pouring the concrete, so the Anasazi sometimes created a rough network of saplings, tied together with bark strips, before applying mud to make an adobe wall. Windows were merely created by omitting the mud from an area (or by the subsequent loss of the mud from a section of the network), leaving some reinforcing willows exposed. Many people in the world have no idea what's inside a wall, and so jailhouse bars do spring to mind.

We camped alongside the creek just below Jailhouse, but the creek was dried up. And so we hiked downstream until finding a seep, and hauled water back to camp. After dinner, I set off across the sloping slabs of sandstone, contouring

The storehouse and kiva under the Perfect Kiva overhang, as seen from the possible observer path to the west. The T-shaped doorway is much shorter than the 150 centimeter height of the average Anasazi male. Rock slabs with grooves from corn grinding (with a flattened stone called a *mano*) are found at several places in this amphitheater. The echos are such that the sounds of the stroke of the mano must have produced an unusual resonance.

around past west-facing Jailhouse Ruin to see the cliffs on the back side of the meander—though the magnificent view upcanyon delayed me somewhat. Once I turned the corner, I was looking downcanyon, to the south, a view that the Anasazi preferred for their cliff dwellings. Tonight the view came with a full moon, rising in the southeast. And soon I stumbled into the most interesting amphitheater that I have yet seen, appropriately named Perfect Kiva.

Except for a small one-room structure along the rear wall with the Anasazi's T-shaped doorway, the only structure is an underground kiva. The space created by this giant overhang looks to me like an enormous ceremonial area, not a dwelling place. As a stage, it is large enough to perform an opera. If you sneeze, as I did, a great resounding crash answers, then rattles around inside the amphitheater. Several of the rocks in the "stage" have a series of deep grooves in them, created by grinding corn there with a smooth rock. The grooves lead to lips that overhang the floor, so there is space beneath for a basket to catch the ground-up corn. There were dozens of these deep grooves; either they did a lot of ceremonial corn grinding at harvest time, or this was also an everyday workspace, a cool place to spend the afternoon when Jailhouse Ruin was too hot.

Several others had joined me by this time, and we explored the kiva itself. At Mesa Verde, one sees kivas that look reconstructed. Perfect Kiva is well named. Its kiva is not centered, being closer to the eastern corner of the alcove; it also is set out well in front, not to the drip line but farther forward than any notion of symmetry might suggest. It is a square subterranean room that several dozen people could conceivably occupy, if no one had to breathe. It has a wooden roof, heavily constructed with a dirt covering, looking from the outside like a raised square of stage—though with a one-person square hole, through which one emerges via a ladder. Or enters.

That ladder hole is also the smokehole. There is a ventilation shaft on the south side, like a proper kiva, but it is primarily to keep the fire going. The fire pit and deflector plate (so that the air sucked down the shaft is deflected upward) are beneath the ladder. Lots of smoke rose from the fire pit. I suspect that the primary function of the fire was to produce a "smoke-filled room," enveloping the newcomer as he descended the ladder.

Even without a fire and smoke, descending the ladder into the kiva is an experience; leaving the moonlit world above, one seems to be entering an entirely different kind of world, insulated from the ordinary and the everyday. It is dark, even after you adapt somewhat, and the dust from the dirt floor smells dry. There are some benches around the walls of many kivas, and often they have some ceremonial niches in the walls. I wasn't able to find the sipapu, the little hole in the floor representing the entry from the underworld, out of which all good Anasazi emerged in the beginning. Somehow, I imagined the kiva itself as the underworld, so striking was the contrast with the moonlit alcove.

Added to this was the sound of a pair of feet tapping on the kiva's roof. Someone's idea of an embellishment, with a typical Indian dance rhythm. The roof doesn't seem to be constructed as a drum but who knows what it sounded like during an Anasazi ceremony.

Such was my second night as a troglodyte. The Anasazi may have lacked television, but their sense of drama was well developed.

THE NEXT MORNING BEFORE BREAKFAST, I RETURNED to the ceremonial stage with camera and pocket transit. Was Perfect Kiva like Split-Level Ruin, situated for a good view of the winter solstice sunrise and sunset?

Again I saw the cliff-dweller's world view: a crescent-shaped piece of blue sky, framed by rock. Was the left corner the southeasterly direction of winter solstice sunrise? No—you could see almost due east when standing near the kiva ladder. Oops.

But the right corner was more promising, a nice candidate for winter solstice sunset: there was a deep V-shaped notch at 13.6° elevation, at a bearing of *226.3°* from true north. That right corner was exactly on the sun's calculated path across the sky on the day of the winter solstice. If you move away from the kiva ladder, the notch changes several degrees (as the V is formed by two rock surfaces at different distances from the observer). For watching winter solstice sunset in the corner notch, the kiva is clearly in the right place if my compass is correct. But the skyline is such that the solstice sun will first set behind a dome on the distant horizon, and then reappear briefly in the V, only to disappear again. On the solstice, if you stand at the right place, it probably does not reappear.

So where would sunrise be, on the winter solstice?

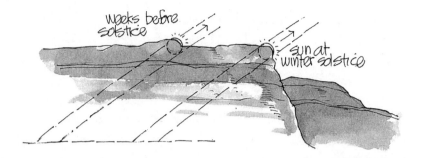

Maybe the Anasazi here used something different than did the Anasazi at Split-Level Ruin, with its convenient crescent corners. In the southeast, you see a ridgeline across the valley when standing at Perfect Kiva's entry. This ridgeline appeared like a staircase, with a series of downsteps as one looks from east around to south. Might one of the downsteps be the location of winter solstice sunrise?

The third downstep is at about *135°* from north and elevated 15° from horizontal: right on the sunrise path through the sky on the shortest day of the year. Furthermore, the step down was rounded and exactly a half-degree tall, just the size of the rising sun. So you could position the sun such that only a thin rim was visible, framed by the rounded downstep for a moment before rising further. It would look much like a solar eclipse ending, all the better for drama.

The pocket transit measurements aren't reliable enough to say that the kiva is exactly the right spot from which to get the crescent view, but it is certainly close. So the solstice sun would rise from the staircased ridgeline, move across the winter sky, set behind that dome, and then reappear briefly in that corner notch (except on the solstice). Within several weeks, the sun would clearly rise atop the rounded downstep, then set above the V-notch without even being obscured first; to keep sunrise obscured into that nice thin rim, you'd have to move right by two paces.

Another kiva with "the right view." I was beginning to think that dramatic qualities might serve as a good guide, at least in the prospecting stage of archaeoastronomy. Physicists have long tended to talk of their theories as "beautiful"

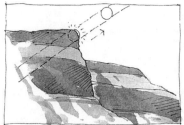

or "elegant"—implying that such aesthetics provided a guide for further exploration ("Any theory that elegant can't be all wrong!") while recognizing that beautiful theories can also be killed by a single ugly fact. Perhaps archaeologists, out prospecting for new sites, ought to consider taking a drama critic along.

THE ALCOVE AT PERFECT KIVA ALSO ALLOWS YOU TO play an interesting game in the weeks before and after the winter solstice, provided that the observer is allowed to move each day. Now ordinarily, given those horizon calendars like the Palisades of the Desert, we think of the observer returning to the same viewpoint morning after morning, seeing the sun rise in different positions, marching south, pausing, and then heading back north. There is a standard observer but the view is of a moving sunrise.

But the observer can also move each morning, just enough to position the sunrise behind the same feature on the horizon—the idea would be to recreate the view each morning by moving sideways a little from the previous morning's position. Moving observer, standard view.

According to my topographic map, the downstep is 161 meters away. That's a nice distance for the pivot point of the observer's seesaw. It means that a month before the solstice, the viewer has to

Corn grinding site. The ears of corn are about as long as an adult finger, miniature by today's standards.

stand outside the alcove to get the sun positioned behind that rounded downstep. Each day, the viewing position moves closer to the kiva. Then for about the last week, the viewer's position doesn't change more than about one meter—and if my compass is right, that standstill viewpoint is the kiva. Finally, the viewpoint starts moving back toward the right side of the alcove.

In some sense, it doesn't matter what definition of sunrise is used, just so that you use the same one each morning— but the place of standstill and turnaround will be different for each definition. Surely they would use the "thin rim" definition here at Perfect Kiva, and I'll bet that's the definition that puts the turnaround at the kiva ladder.

I began to think of the Perfect Kiva alcove as a giant measuring instrument, and of the kiva as the end of the scale, the magic place where the Sun Priest stands still for a week before turning around.

Forgotten Kiva is unusually large (note people at *right*) and located under an enormous overhang, which has protected its roof and entry ladder from the weather over the millennium since its construction. Great kivas may be twice as large.

6

||||||||||||||||

Sightlines
to Somewhere

To the extent that naturalism is restricted as a philosophy, so supernaturalism is expanded. There is nothing in heaven or earth that cannot be explained by supernatural means. That concomitant of ignorance, omniscience, is one of the striking characteristics of primitive peoples. The less a people knows, in the naturalistic sense, the more they seem to know, and can think they know, by employing supernaturalism. And the concomitant of knowledge, control, follows the same route. Little attempt is made to control nature by naturalistic means, but a great deal of social time goes into the attempt at control by supernatural means. . . . Every "thing" in nature [is said to have] a spirit which not only is the explanation for its characteristics, but also provides a means for human beings to influence it.

the anthropologist ELMAN R. SERVICE, *1966*

Camping out that night after the hike up out of Anasazi Valley, I discovered an interesting use for a north-facing alcove that we'd visited (where, alas, we had to rebury some human bones that were scattered by thieves in their search for Anasazi pots). You can use a north-facing overhang to point at the "axis of the universe." Naturally I thought of this use too late to check out that particular alcove.

Particularly if it is really dark and there is a canyon rim to the east of you, the stars seem to pop out, one by one, in the dry desert air. While it is really the earth rotating, a flat-earth viewpoint might reasonably assume that the heavens were rotating. And there is one star that doesn't move very much these days, not more than 1-2° during the night. Polaris seems to be the immobile point around which the heavens spin, the axis of the universe. There was a tall tree just north of where I camped, a dead tree that looked as if it had been struck by lightning in centuries past. I walked around on the mesa until Polaris stood atop the pinnacle of the tree. Now I had a pointer to the "axis of the universe."

I went back to camp and got my sleeping bag, bringing

it back to this spot, laying it out so that I faced the tree. Whenever I woke up that night, Polaris was still atop the tree (actually rotating in a tiny circle around it). But the other stars had shifted quite a lot, seemingly rotating around that treetop. The handle of the Little Dipper, *Ursa minor*, indicated the time, in effect. The "pointer stars" of the Big Dipper, *Ursa major*, are even easier to locate, drawing an imaginary pointer to Polaris. Both handles were like the hour hand of a clock. By comparing a handle's angle relative to the tree with what the angle was at twilight, I could estimate what hour of the night it was. Do you suppose that's where clock hands come from? (Shadows from sundials are the usual candidate, but they don't usually rotate in a complete circle as the stars do.)

I thought back to that north-facing alcove—and wondered if it might have a notch in its overhang that would point to the same place in the sky, if you were to lie in the Right Spot. North-facing overhangs also might have summer solstice sightlines in their corners and notches. Of course, the Right Spot wouldn't have been Polaris back in Anasazi days, with Polaris rotating in a more noticeable circle (about 6° radius) about the Right Spot. I haven't heard much about the archaeology of north-facing alcoves, except that they were used as burial places. An honored position for honored dead in the Right Spot? The Pueblo peoples do have strong traditions about an underworld that is six months in advance of the real world, which a life-afterlife/summer-winter antithesis would fit right into. I think that, if I were an Anasazi trying to piece together a story of the universe, this might all seem to make perfect sense. Or am I just extrapolating too much? It took hours before I finally fell asleep.

And then I woke up hours later (according to my handy clock), thinking about tepees, those conical tents of the plains Indians (and various tribes are known to practice star-watching from inside ceremonial tents). Tepee smokeholes ought to have a view of Polaris too, if you could lie on the floor in the right place. That almost caused me to get up and go pacing around. But I discovered the problem with that theory even before leaving the warm confines of the sleeping bag: the tepees couldn't be tall and narrow unless they were at Canadian latitudes; the farther south you go, the broader the base of the tepee would need to be, if anyone was to see Polaris out of its smokehole. At Anasazi latitudes, the tepee would need a radius that was somewhat more than its height. A little squat—not the usual shape of a tepee. Another good idea, spoiled by trigonometry. But most north-facing over-hangs in Anasazi Valley are probably deep enough so that an observer could see Polaris in a notch in the overhang.

MESA VERDE IN SOUTHERN COLORADO HAS THE MOST famous of Anasazi cliff dwellings (if I discover that someone has never heard of the Anasazi, explaining that the Anasazi were the people who built Mesa Verde always provides in-stant comprehension). I wondered whether the Mesa Verde kivas had solstice sightlines, too. It was only a day's drive to find out.

Even from the map, the prospect of discovering solstice sightlines was discouraging because most Mesa Verde al-coves (Balcony House is the major exception) face west or southwest, not south in the manner of the cliff dwellings in Anasazi Valley. An observer back in an alcove that faces to the west would not see the winter sun until afternoon. Such alcoves certainly must have been cold in the winter (and they often got the hot afternoon sun in the summer, as some alcoves are not very deep). Chapin Mesa just doesn't seem to have any deep natural alcoves facing south at which to apply the architectural principles that the Anasazi clearly knew all about, judging from other cliff dwellings. Perhaps the An-asazi considered Mesa Verde a second-rate building site.

So, I did not expect to see solstice sunrise alignments in a crescent corner. From back in the alcove, the sun rises in the afternoon, *descending* from the top of the overhang! Might a kiva at Mesa Verde, nonetheless, be situated for "a good view" of winter solstice sunset? But, at Mesa Verde, one cannot simply go and look ("Write an application and wait a year while we consider it," insisted the head archaeologist). I decided to do a quick preliminary survey from the mesa tops to the west. (An important element of modern scientific strategy, surely not faced by prehistoric protoscientists, is, "Do preliminary observations before spending time at writing long applications.")

Cliff Palace, the most famous restored pueblo, can be viewed from a tourist overlook that is on a finger of the mesa top just across a little valley to the southwest of the alcove. And, I realized, the inhabitants would have seen their sunsets right over where the tourist overlook now stands. If tourists a thousand years ago had stood there too, they might have blocked the view of the winter solstice sunset from those kivas inside the alcoves—just as Indians standing in the window at Delicate Arch could have turned the stage spotlight on and off.

I didn't need permission to wander around that finger of the mesa. And so I endeavored to find exactly the right place to stand, just to see if it corresponded to some notch in the cliff edge or ruin on the mesa top. Standing on the mesa rim, I had to look 5° down to the kivas in Cliff Palace, so that a shaman at a kiva ladder would have had to look 5° up to where I stood. The sun's path through the southwest sky on the winter solstice passes through 5° elevation when at a bearing of about *236°*. Facing northeast, I took back-bearings and promptly maneuvered myself to the exact spot on the mesa top where their winter solstice sunset would occur (so that the *back* end of my compass needle pointed to *236°*), the spot on the rim that the sun would appear to touch, viewed from their kivas.

And that place on the rim was unexceptional—it had no notch. There were no ruins nearby. There was no hole in the rock, no nothing. Well, perhaps these people liked summer solstice sunsets instead, and so I tried the sightline at *296°*. Nothing. Remembering the moonrise and moonset extremes at Stonehenge, I even tried them. Nothing again. I tried at

Spruce House Ruin, but nothing there either. I couldn't find a single half-promising sightline in my preliminary survey of all the cliff dwellings on the usual tourist route around Mesa Verde.

That quick survey saved me a week of paperwork and a second trip to southern Colorado. Maybe some ruin has a solstice sightline—the maps aren't good enough to rule that out—and maybe some kiva had a mesa-top marker that did not endure. But within several hours, I convinced myself that the *typical* Anasazi kiva at Mesa Verde does not have a demarcated view of a solstice sunset (and certainly not of a solstice sunrise). Hmm. Are these ugly facts, or have I merely overgeneralized?

BETATAKIN AND ANOTHER GREAT ALCOVE, KEET SEEL, are located in Arizona within Navajo National Monument, about 60 kilometers east of the Grand Canyon. They are far more impressive in appearance than Mesa Verde.

Navajo National Monument lies about 20 kilometers north of the tracks for the automated coal train that Edward Abbey described in *The Monkey Wrench Gang*. Betatakin is on a high forested plateau just east of the White Mesa; gullies cut down into it, just as at Anasazi Valley, but not quite as deeply. Still, it is perfect country for alcoves under overhangs.

Betatakin is an alcove in which the Anasazi built a village starting in A.D. 1250. We know that from the trees they cut to build their roofs and ladders. They abandoned Betatakin in A.D. 1279, after only one generation. As the thirteenth century ended, so did the great cliff-dwelling phase of the Anasazi. The decline of Betatakin occurred about the same time as that of Mesa Verde—indeed, the distinctive Anasazi culture itself also dwindled away over the next half century. It is often said that the Anasazi people themselves disappeared and, while the population decline makes that somewhat true, it is really the distinct culture that ended then, in the merger with non-Anasazi tribes that led to the pueblo culture.

A 29-year-long history provides the archaeologists at Betatakin with a brief snapshot in time; Old World archaeologists often have to contend with a series of occupations, their layers somewhat smeared together in time because someone reused materials from an earlier construction, or dug down into an older layer to bury something or create a foundation. But Anasazi archaeologists are used to such brief snapshots—a great many Anasazi sites were inhabited for less than a century, and never reused.

GOVERNMENT NAMES FOR ANASAZI SITES ARE USUALLY wildly inaccurate. As a name, Navajo National Monument has some minor logic: The Navajo may not have constructed the cliff dwellings but the land was later a part of the Navajo Indian Reservation. An Anasazi site in northwestern New Mexico is called Aztec National Monument, a truly gross misnomer as the Aztecs were never anywhere near these latitudes. The first thing that the park rangers have to explain at national monuments in the Southwest is that the names are wrong, a product of anthropological ignorance back in the days before the land was set aside—and officially named— by an Act of Congress.

No major Anasazi site is officially named for the Anasazi—not even "Anasazi Valley." I've created a *nom de guerre* because of its fragile nature, though I haven't changed the names of the ruins themselves, which are clearly described in the archaeological literature. Most Anasazi sites are totally unprotected against looters, so archaeologists guard their maps. You can't buy the good topographic maps at many national park visitor centers anymore. That policy may cut down on the casual hiker taking home something, but the professional looters have often been in the business for generations, father introducing son to backcountry sites, a collection of the best maps probably being a family heirloom. Since the Antiquities Act of 1979 made looting ruins a matter of federal law even when done on private land, there have been some notable prosecutions of thieves, some of

whom held public office in Utah and had escaped state pros-
ecution for years.

A HIKE DOWN THE PATH BEHIND THE NAVAJO NATIONAL
Monument's visitor center brings one to a view of Betatakin
from the cliff top across the canyon from it: one's first impression is that it is enormous, a giant bandshell in an orange
cliff, suitable for an orchestra of a thousand. Unlike the cliff-
dwellings at Mesa Verde, which almost fill the alcove, the
building sites at Betatakin occupy only the bottom fifth of
the height of the alcove. There is no lack of headroom.

Betatakin has a steep, sloping floor and the foundations
of the rooms are cemented onto this potentially slippery
slope. An area in the middle of the ruins has slid away
totally—and I don't mean that the building slipped off its
angled foundation, but that the underlying slab of rock itself
has slid downhill. This erosional pattern—along with sections of the alcove's roof collapsing occasionally—most
likely created the bandshell. And so, because of the slope,
Betatakin's layout is nothing at all like the one permitted by
Perfect Kiva's flat floor.

I took the first tour of the day, pocket transit in pocket,
following the park ranger up the valley. Betatakin looks
enormous as you approach it from below, every bit as impressive as the view from the high overlook across the valley.
After exploring all of the ruins on the usual route and searching in vain for the characteristic kiva shape and ventilation
shaft, I finally asked the ranger. Only the kiva's foundations
remain, he explained, just below the diagonal path that allows access to the east end's upper stories. And so I picked
my way carefully over to where he indicated, one of the
steeper slopes and—one might think—not a very desirable
building site for such an important structure. I sat down on
the trail, probably the access route to the kiva ladder in the
old days, and pulled out the pocket transit.

The southwest corner, where bandshell meets the distant horizon, is not anywhere close to winter solstice sunset.

Above, Looking west inside the huge alcove of Betatakin, the kiva is seen at lower center, appearing below the flight of rock-hewn steps. The kiva entrance was presumably in its roof and reached by the transverse path visible just above the kiva.

Left, Looking southeast from the steps, the kiva walls are seen in the foreground, attached to the steep slope. Park ranger is standing on the path below the kiva.

Nor is the southeast crescent corner near the winter sunrise. It is far too low to be on the sun's path through the sky on the shortest day of the year. Had I struck out again?

I noticed, however, an interesting ledge in the overhang, which forms a notch, and so I measured it too. It is at *139.5°* from north and elevated 17.5°, very close indeed to the sun's path on the winter solstice. So the rising sun would be framed by that notch—at least, if you stand at the kiva. Could the little step be a symbolic substitute for a crescent corner?

Betatakin's kiva makes a total of three kivas with a special view of winter solstice sunrise—special, at least, compared with other structures in their village. As I hiked out, I speculated: Mosques face toward Mecca, could kivas face the sun's path through the sky on the winter solstice? (Well, except for those kivas built by the poor relatives at Mesa Verde.) I could see that I was going to have to collect some more kivas.

AFTER A COOL DRINK OF WATER BACK AT THE VISITOR center, I was all set to continue on to Keet Seel (Navajo National Monument's other great alcove) as soon as possible, to see if its kiva was also in the right place for a special solstice view. I looked at the archaeologists' map of the Keet Seel ruins and, to my dismay, there were dozens of kivas! This is a case of "too much of a good thing." They can't *all* have solstice views. Even if a few did, who would believe my kiva-siting theory, when I had so many kivas to select among?

I was immediately reminded of the cogent criticism of the sightlines of famous ruins in Egypt, Europe, and Central America, the ones that are supposedly oriented to point at a certain star. Because so many stars are packed into the night sky, any given sightline *always* points at one star or another. Unless one has strong independent evidence for a people favoring a particular star, saying that a sightline through an ancient ruin points to where Sirius rises is like saying that the view out my bedroom window was created to point to the rising of Sirius. Every sightline points somewhere and every few minutes, a different star moves into the sightline. Such stellar sightline claims are not very convincing to anyone who thinks in terms of modern control experiments, of the probability that a sightline could be thus-and-so merely by chance. Have I fallen into the same trap with kiva sightlines?

While sipping coffee in the visitor center, I asked myself whether my Betatakin sightline from the kiva to the prominent notch in the overhang happened to point to the sun's winter solstice path just by chance, that the Anasazi just happened to build the kiva there for some other reason but it turned out to have this nice view. The first uncertainty is that the sun has a finite size and I don't know whether the Anasazi liked to sight using the top of the sun, or its left edge, or its right edge, or its bottom. So there is 0.5° uncertainty, just from that—a half degree of freedom to fit a square peg into a round hole, as it were.

The sun's size is not the only "loose fit" in this business. The second bit of slack is that there is a span of about 60° between the northeastern summer solstice sunrise (at *60°* from north with a horizontal horizon) and the southeasterly winter solstice sunrise (at *120°*). And as I move around within an alcove, the angles keep changing to the various horizon features. What, one must ask, are the chances of my finding a viewpoint at which a particular horizon feature in that general direction comes to lie between *60.0* and *60.5°*? Or between *119.5* and *120.0°*?

You could fit 120 objects of the sun's apparent diameter side-by-side into that sector, so the chance of the sun hitting any one *0.5°* segment is 0.8 percent. That is the chance of a randomly selected sightline being usable for winter solstice. There is also a 0.8 percent chance of the sightline being used for summer solstice sunrise, since I'll shout *eureka* if it hits either one of them. So the probabilities total 1.6 percent that I could pick an easterly feature *by chance* that would work for one or another of the solstice sunrises. Someone, I groaned, should do this analysis for Stonehenge and Avebury view-points too, all those dozens of stones to choose from, each with two sides.

Now, suppose that there are *two* interesting horizon features along the eastern horizon from which to choose—as there are down at Betatakin: the usual crescent corner, and that prominent notch higher on the overhang (the one that seems to work pretty well for winter solstice sunrise). Having two candidates doubles my choices, doubles the risk that I'll find something just by chance, rather than because the Anasazi liked to build their kivas where there's a solstice view. Two convenient sightlines mean I've got a 3.2 percent chance of having one of them fit my summer-or-winter-solstice-sunrise hypothesis. And since I can pick and choose from the western sky in the same way, double that if there are two interesting features along the southwest-to-northwest horizon. We're up to 6.4 percent. I don't even want to think about bumpy skylines such as the Palisades of the Desert, with a dozen notches rather than two.

Two candidates in the east, and two in the west, gives me one chance in sixteen that I'm fooling myself about Anasazi intentions, should I find a single solstice sightline from a particular viewpoint. Most scientists won't accept chances that big as "significant," sufficiently different from the it's-all-random alternative. Even a one-in-a-hundred "chance level" can cause eyebrows to be raised.

So single sightlines from single sites, by themselves, are not going to be persuasive. They offer too much "creative freedom," when what you want is to be constrained by the facts, to be forced to say, "That's the *only* possible answer." My opinion of half the archaeoastronomy literature took a nosedive—so much of it could just be wishful thinking, a clever modern idea imposed on the site and tailored to fit. We want something as unequivocal as a suit of armor, but what we typically get in archaeoastronomy is a situation about as flexible as a bolt of *stretch* fabric, which fits anything.

I cheered up after realizing that, while my pessimism may be appropriate for analyzing one site at a time, were we to survey many Anasazi kivas and they *typically* had winter solstice sunrise sightlines, then that would be pretty persuasive that solstice sunrise views were important kiva-siting considerations—a *pattern* is one way to get around the daunting odds posed by data from only one site.

ANOTHER WAY TO ESCAPE THE DEPRESSING PROBABILIties would be to discover two solstice sightlines intersecting at a kiva. The special viewpoints at both Split-Level Ruin and Perfect Kiva were in about the right place for *both* sunrise and sunset at winter solstice.

If you can pick the second sightline without being constrained by the first one, their individual probabilities multiply to give the probability of both happening by chance. With two candidate sightlines from the eastern horizon to choose between, and another two from the western, the chance of being in the right place by chance for two solstice sightlines is about 3.2 percent of 3.2 percent, or 0.1 percent chance of both happening randomly from the same viewpoint.

And that one-in-a-thousand probability would apply to a winter solstice sunrise and a summer solstice sunset seen from a single viewpoint. The chances of *both* sunrise and sunset on the *same* solstice having sightlines through my viewpoint is even smaller. This makes sites with two same-solstice sightlines pretty rare by chance, and far more believable than a single sightline that fits one of the varied possibilities. That an intersection should also contain the Anasazi's most unusual building type also improves believability.

ACOMA PUEBLO REMINDS ME OF NOTHING SO MUCH as King Herod's mountaintop fortress overlooking the Dead Sea. Both Acoma and Masada are solitary, flat-topped mountains—a mesa, to use the Spanish word for table—and capped with buildings.

Although it is fortified, Herod's mesa is basically your standard Roman winter palace, the first century B.C. version of going south for the winter (Herodion, atop a breast-shaped hill south of Jerusalem and east of Bethlehem, is the summer version, up in the cooler Judean Hills with breezes from the Mediterranean). Masada is one of the best places in the world to see a Roman palace, for the simple reason that another town was never built atop it. Deserts have their virtues (less desirable sites, and a dry climate that preserves) and so archaeologists spend disproportionate amounts of their time at desert sites, dealing with hot dust.

Acoma Pueblo is still inhabited. It has the same desert setting as Masada, though without the view up the northern extension of the East African Rift Valley that Herod had. The Rift is part of that superfault line that extends from South Africa to Turkey, and the reason why Jericho has four major earthquakes every century (which still cause its walls to come tumbling down).

Acoma lacks the opulence of Masada, whose construction and ongoing water supply were supported by slave labor. Acoma's problem was the reverse: The Spanish regularly hauled its young people away into slavery for all of that church construction that needed manual labor. But Acoma survived in its low-budget way, and stands today as a living monument to how determined Native American hunter-gatherers can make a go of marginal farming in a country where the non-native Americans seemingly cannot live without importing gasoline, electricity, and water.

Acoma is one of several pueblos that you encounter when driving west on the interstate highway from Albu-querque, New Mexico. Driving south from the freeway exit, the first sight is a tall mesa that appears uninhabited. It is sacred to the people of Acoma, the topic of many legends (I don't know what their name for it is; their tourist brochure says that *others* call it "Enchanted Mesa"). It rises about 30 stories above a flat desert floor in the midst of a wide valley. I wondered if there were ceremonial sites atop it with solstice

views, but the archaeologists seem not to have been successful in persuading the tribe to permit surveys; the tribe does
not even permit hikers to visit.

To the south of Enchanted Mesa is another mesa, somewhat larger. Atop it are many buildings, including the bell
tower of a church (the San Esteban del Rey Mission was built
in 1629-1640, after Catholic missionaries followed the Spanish soldiers into the area). This is Acoma, first inhabited back
in early Anasazi times, nearly two thousand years ago, with
an influx of people from the Mesa Verde area about A.D.
1300. Coronado's army visited it in 1540, describing it as

> One of the strongest ever seen, because the city was
> built on a high rock. The ascent was so difficult that we
> repented climbing to the top. The houses are three and
> four stories high. The people are of the same type as [the
> Zuni] and they have abundant supplies of maize, beans,
> and turkeys. . . .

Like Masada, Acoma has a rocky path leading from base
to top, which passed through easily guarded "choke points,"
as soldiers would say today. A twentieth-century addition
has been a blacktop road; fortunately, tourists' cars are not
allowed up it. Tourists stop at the Acoma visitor center at the
bottom, look at the museum, and then ride up in a school bus
with a native guide.

When I was there, Indian corn was being prepared for a
festival, amidst much workaday ceremony by the old men.
Imagine a group of local, hardworking farmers whom you
know, gathered together for a communal festivity with religious overtones, and you will have the general feeling of the
ceremony. But further imagine a farmer gesturing with each
ear of corn, shaking it in each of their four cardinal directions, then up to the skies, lastly down to the earth. Whether
or not cardinal directions are important for eclipse forecasting, these farmers think them important for harvesting the
corn and setting aside the seed corn for next year. In the

Pueblo traditions, religion, agriculture, and the calendar of the seasons are intertwined. The use of solstice directions for cardinal directions is common in the more western pueblos, though the Christian influence has seemingly resulted in many of the eastern pueblos converting to north-east-south-west.

A few big pools of muddy water stood atop the mesa, thanks to recent thundershowers. These catch basins are the source of water for most purposes. Children played in them, animals wandered through them to cool off, and the water had come to look quite muddy. Occasionally, a child arrived to fill a bucket or jug (the mud settles to the bottom of the container, if you wait long enough). Most households now haul up their drinking water from purer sources below, but water for other purposes still comes from these old-fashioned cisterns. Until recently, no one understood how disease was spread through such water supplies. Cholera epidemics in New York City (as late as 1866) finally led to the construction of covered water mains to import water from outlying water-sheds, and other expensive municipal investments to export wastes in covered sewers. It is amazing just how far Western civilization progressed without such a beginner's under-standing of epidemic diseases. At Acoma, they got a head start on the export half of the problem: The outhouses are located on the edge of the cliff.

Not far from the natural cistern stands the mission church with its Spanish-style bell towers; a European-style graveyard stretches out to the edge of the mesa. It is bor-dered by a few trees, looking strangely out of place, and surely surviving only because of constant watering. A little touch of Spain, adapted to the desert Southwest in minor ways. The Pueblo Indians of New Mexico who adopted Christianity modified that religion in many ways, blending in ancient festivals with modern ones. For instance, there is a festival just a few days after the summer solstice (just as Christmas is a few days after the winter solstice). Acoma is the westernmost of the Rio Grande pueblos, and considered a somewhat intermediate case, lacking certain Spanish influences seen in the pueblos nearer the Rio Grande Valley.

Inside, it is a poor church, though one that reveals what a feat of construction it was for the Acoma of three centuries ago. Anasazi, it isn't. The view outside its doors is splendid, stretching across the valley below to the mountains.

Sorting out the old and the new is a challenge in the pueblos of New Mexico because of the priests' doings over the last four centuries, plus the Mexican influence. In addition, for the last century, all have been surrounded by the twentieth-century culture of European, African, and Asian origins. Farther west into what is now Arizona, the priests and the settlers were slower in coming, and so the Hopi may have maintained more of the original Anasazi culture. By comparing common elements among the Hopi, the Zuni, and the Rio Grande Pueblos, and contrasting them with Anasazi archaeology, one can get some imperfect idea of what the Anasazi culture was like.

BANDELIER NATIONAL MONUMENT IS IN NORTHERN New Mexico, just above the Rio Grande River, and the cliff dwellings there are quite different than in Anasazi Valley or Mesa Verde. The rock is a soft lava, and one sees many holes drilled into the stone faces to support roof beams. While the cliffs that overlooked narrow valley floors were popular, there are also outlying areas that look more like Acoma and Masada: mesas with cliff dwellings along their southern faces, with long views.

Tsankawi, overlooking the Rio Grande valley, is my favorite example, partly because it has real *cave*-dwellings, not merely dwellings built under a cliff overhang. There were some large blowholes in the lava, creating various nooks and crannies in the cliff face. And the lava is soft enough that some nooks were enlarged to form nice rooms with shaped doorways.

And there is a square cave, no less. In the westernmost cave on the path, they squared up the room and plastered the lower half of the walls in the manner that one sees in kivas. Over the T-shaped Anasazi doorway, with its notches for a lintel (probably a "curtain-rod" pole that held an animal skin to cover the opening), is a long, narrow hole drilled through the rock (perhaps a natural hole that was reamed out). This opening faces south, and at midday a spotlight of sunlight moves across the floor of the room. In midwinter, the spotlight would pass along the foot of the back wall of the room (so far as one can tell, without knowing how deep a layer of dirt now covers the original floor).

HOPI INDIAN RESERVATION IS CENTERED ON THREE large mesas in northeastern Arizona. The Hopi's mesas bear little relation to well-defined round or rectangular "tables" such as Acoma or Masada. Rather, they are southern "fingers" of Black Mesa to their north, peninsulas in the sky once again. At the southern edge of each finger, the land falls away to the south, creating a splendid vista. But elsewhere, the high land is undulating and the views are limited. It is mostly dry, high desert; the interesting features are along its edges.

The hillsides force upward some of the warm, moist air that blows northwest from the Gulf of Mexico. As this air cools, it becomes too saturated to hold onto its moisture. The summer rainfall from the monsoons is why the Anasazi probably liked this place and other such south-facing hills. Such hillsides get what rain there is in this land of low rainfall and recurrent drought. The Hopi farmers grow their blue corn in streambeds where the water is channeled; whenever one drives over a little gully, one can look down from the bridge and probably spot a plot of Hopi corn, each plant carefully tended by hand. The streambed may look dry, but the sandy bottom is likely to have some water beneath the sunbaked surface. The hillsides are a more chancy proposition, and the Hopi farmer plays his chances in an interesting way.

While the sides of the mesas catch the summer rainfall more reliably than the lowlands and the high country, a Hopi farmer will plant some crops at the bottom of a mesa, some halfway up, and the rest up on top. The top fields will get the rainfall that precipitates out as monsoon clouds drifting north are pushed up to high altitudes each summer day. In a bad year, the fields at the base will get little rainfall and the crops there will fail; the plots halfway up will be stunted, but the top fields will still yield a crop. In a good year, all three sets of fields will prosper. It's called "spreading your bets," a practice often ignored by modern farmers who specialize in one high-paying crop and then suffer the pests and diseases promoted by the monoculture conditions (the Irish potato famine comes to mind).

NO ISOLATED DWELLINGS DOT THE HOPI'S LAND, AS one would typically see in the Navajo's land that surrounds the Hopi reservation. The Hopi mostly live in compact villages, and hike out to tend their scattered plots (though the pickup truck has served to shorten the hike these days).

One thing that the Navajo did not borrow from the Pueblo Indians was this tendency to cluster; I have a hard time imagining a group of Navajo families taking up residence in the confines of a cliff-dwelling, though it would probably seem familiar and comfortable to the Hopi (though a little odd, having a dome over one's homes). The Navajo's tendency is to spread out, to establish themselves in distant gullies at the end of a long rutted road, build a hogan, and raise a large family there (one is reminded of the European pioneers settling the West).

This has had implications for population size, and is one reason why the notion of the Navajo and Hopi sharing a "joint use area" surrounding the Hopi Reservation proper didn't work out (it finally had to be partitioned, causing some Navajo "pioneers" to be evicted). The Navajo are expansionistic, while—one tends to hypothesize—the Pueblo people's population stabilizes around the size that a traditional village site can accommodate.

Though there are some exceptions, Hopi villages are

often located on those long southern fingers of Black Mesa. Walpi stands high above the highway that skirts the southern edge of First Mesa, looking like a knife-edge version of an Italian hill town such as Assisi. Acoma has cliffs all around, but those of Hopi are half again as high, totaling about 45 stories tall. One suspects that the Hopi built atop these wind-swept, waterless ridges not so much for practicality but because these places were somewhat like those where their legendary ancestors lived, settings embedded into the An-asazi cosmology.

THE HOPI'S CALENDAR APPEARS, AT FIRST GLANCE, TO be the usual amalgam of lunar and solar events that characterized calendars before our modern calendar simplified things somewhat. Various North American Indians learned to add a thirteenth lunar month every three years to bring the calendar back into synchronization with the seasons.

While the phases of the moon are merely footnotes to a modern calendar, they used to be an integral part of things, and still are used in setting the dates of religious festivals. The day on which Easter occurs, for example, is the first Sunday following the first full moon after the spring equinox. Thus it is first keyed to the solar cycle of the seasons (the equinox must have happened), then to the monthly maturation of the moon, and finally to the notion of when the week begins (and weeks are not keyed to anything, Sunday drifting with respect to full moon, New Year's Day, the equinoxes, etc.). The Easter arrangement sounds suspiciously like a compromise solution to an ancient argument between opposing religious factions.

Most Hopi festivals are keyed to a similar combination of solar and lunar events—but their highest festival, Soyal, is about as close to the day of the winter solstice as they can make it by observation of the sunrise and sunset on the horizon. The date of Soyal each year is determined by a village elder called the *tawa-mongwi* or Sun Chief. Standing at a favorite observation spot on Second Mesa, he carefully observes sunset over the San Francisco Peaks, surely the most prominent landmark visible from their high plateau. When sunset reaches a characteristic position about ten days before its extreme southwestern position, he announces that Soyal is ten days hence, and preparations begin. The Zuni tell this story about the first Sun Priest:

> The man who went to the Sun was made Pekwin. The Sun told him, "When you get home you will be Pekwin and I will be your father. Make meal offerings to me. Come to the edge of the town every morning and pray to me. Every evening go to the shrine at Matsaki and pray. At the end of the year when I come to the south, watch me closely; and in the middle of the year in the same month, when I reach the farthest point on the right hand, watch me closely." "All right." He came home and learned for three years, and he was made Pekwin. The first year at the last month of the year he watched the Sun closely, but his calculations were early by thirteen days. Next year he was early by twenty days. He studied again. The next year his calculations were two days late. In eight years he was able to time the turning of the sun exactly. The people made prayer sticks and held ceremonies in the winter and in the summer, at just the time of the turning of the sun.
>
> from RUTH BENEDICT, *Zuni Mythology, 1969*

The solstice positions on the horizon are known to all Zuni and Hopi, as they are the directions to which all others are referenced. They play an important role in rituals and prayer. Just as a Catholic celebrating the mass will point to the four ends of a symbolic cross, so a Hopi celebrant will make an offering of grain to each of the six directions: summer solstice sunset, winter sunset, winter sunrise, and summer sunrise, then to the zenith above and the nadir below—just as I saw at that harvest ceremony at Acoma. Knowing the solstice directions on the horizon, wherever you may be, is part of being Hopi.

Sun watching goes on year-round, not just near the solstices. You can see a big advantage to using a horizon-based calendar for an agricultural people, especially when it comes to judging planting time. Late frosts in the spring may kill vulnerable new sprouts and frosts are again a problem as harvest time approaches. The frost-free growing season for Hopi corn is about 120-130 days and, because of the altitude, that means that there are no weeks to spare in many places: Planting at the right time is crucial. Too late means having to harvest when the ears of corn lack full maturity; too early means that the frost may kill the sprouts. As even amateur gardeners know, sniffing the air on the first fine day of spring is not the way to decide when to plant. The accumulated wisdom of farmers had to be keyed to something besides the phases of the moon, which are ten days earlier the next year. Obviously, one wants to key to the cycle of the seasons, i.e., the sun.

We naturally think that counting 365 days a year should solve the problem. But no law says that the earth must rotate on its axis at a rate that fits with the rotation around the sun. The earth rotates 365.24 times on its axis during each orbit about the sun (the earth used to spin faster on its axis, getting in more than 400 days in a year, but the rotation has slowed down since Precambrian times, thanks to the back-and-forth motion of tides). Leap years are one way to correct for this lack of an integer number of days in a round trip around the sun, but were not invented until 46 B.C. A far simpler calendar, with none of these complications, is to use the position of the sunrise on the horizon. It is perfect for determining the time to plant.

Even if you do not have a convenient mountain peak to mark sunrise on the right day of the year, you can construct rock cairns to the east of your front door: Each year, you make a pile of rocks (a shrine, if you like) on the day that you start planting, located right on the path from your front door to the sunrise. If it turns out to be a bad year for corn, you go out and kick down the offending cairn. For the rock piles, it's

117

the survival of the fittest. After a decade of this, only the cairns for the good years will remain—and then you can start using sunrise behind the tallest cairn as your indicator of when it is best to start planting.

Since horizon calendars have none of the drift problems of lunar-solar calendars or our current day-counting calendars, this "primitive" calendar seems quite trouble-free, perfect for a settled people who do not travel very far from home. Judging by the way agricultural instructions are embedded in Pueblo religions, such directions became part of religious tradition.

> *The Hopi have no real professional astronomers, just as they have no narrow specialists in meteorology, agriculture, or theology. Instead, they have elders, widely educated in the ritually transmitted wisdom of clan and tribe.*
>
> *the historian* STEPHEN C. MCCLUSKEY, *1982*

THE NEXT WINTER, I RETURNED A FEW DAYS AFTER the solstice and photographed Betatakin from the visitor's overlook across the canyon, from which I first admired the bandshell shape. When I arrived, the sun was already casting an oblique shadow of the roofline; it fell diagonally across the sloping floor of the bandshell. The shadowline clearly showed the corner-shaped notch, far back up behind the ruins. I watched the notch slowly sweep down, crossing the alcove as the sun rose in the sky and moved south.

I am happy to report that the notch's shadow passed directly through the kiva (it's always nice to verify that your observation technique and computer program are not fooling you). Winter solstice observers at the kiva would indeed

The huge bandshell-shaped alcove at Betatakin, showing the sunrise shadow of the pillar at right falling across the kiva near the winter solstice. Only the west wall of the kiva is visible, slightly to the left of center. Note the shadow's notch, indicating that an observer at the kiva would have seen the sun framed by the top of the pillar.

have seen the sun rise near that notch of the overhang. I doubt that they would have framed the sun atop the step—when the sun is so high in the sky, it is simply too bright to look at. Perhaps they obscured the rising sun behind the outcrop, in the manner of Perfect Kiva's rounded downstep. And side-stepped their way along that east-west path to the kiva entry, in the weeks before winter solstice? So Betatakin's kiva definitely has a solstice view, even if the crescent corners of sky fail to celebrate the winter solstice in the manner of Split-Level Ruin.

Building a kiva to align with winter solstice is not simply analogous to building a mosque to face Mecca; yes, the architecture is what remains, but it was presumably part of a process in the same way that a scientific apparatus is part of a scientific practice. The priests have a lot of observational work to do for the winter solstice. That the Sun Priest is expected to schedule the celebrations on exactly the right day has an interesting consequence: If his prediction is inaccurate, he is blamed for everything that goes wrong during the following year. If a child dies, or the rains don't come, or the crops fail, it's his fault. The Sun Priest may not be executed by an unhappy emperor, as happened to those Chinese astronomers who failed to predict the solar eclipse in 2134 B.C., but he's still very motivated to avoid mistakes in observations and calculations.

And how might someone have known that Soyal was celebrated on the wrong day? Just use some other horizon feature that the sun passes several weeks before the solstice and count the days until the sun returns to it; the solstice turnaround should have been exactly midway through the period. Division is not necessary. Just create a string of beads with the passing days, using a special bead for the day Soyal was celebrated. When the necklace is completed by the return of the sun to the horizon feature, hold the string by the Soyal bead so that the two halves dangle down. There should be an equal length of beads on each side, if Soyal were correctly celebrated.

Such were the prehistoric motivations for doing better and better science? A little ability to predict the future, even something as routine as the turnaround of the seasons, has enormous consequences for the role of the prophet-scientist in society—it starts a clock running, in the minds of others, and often a scoreboard. Becoming a prophet carries both opportunities and risks.

We think that the Sun-watcher is not a very good man. He missed some places, he was wrong last year. . . . All the people think that is why we had so much cold this winter and no snow.

the Hopi Indian CROW WING, *1925*

7

||||||||||||||

Cornering the Sun
in a Canyon

Both when they are right and when they are wrong, [ideas] are more powerful than is commonly understood. Indeed the world is ruled by little else. Practical men, who believe themselves to be exempt from any intellectual influences, are usually the slaves of some defunct economist.

JOHN MAYNARD KEYNES

An idea about an idea—that's what I seem to be following around the ruins. Or, at least, a hunch. Civilizations are built on ideas, and to understand ourselves, we need a better notion about how hunter-gatherers got the idea of giving up their wandering life-style and settling down to agriculture and occupational specialties. That's what the Anasazi did, starting several thousand years ago.

My hunch seems, on the face of it, to be about such matters as what the Anasazi's part-time architects considered "a good view" or a dramatic setting. Or what their priests might have found worth celebrating, such as a solstice. But if I can somehow connect such things to eclipses, there is the prospect of explaining how the local shaman evolved into the emperor's astronomer, how priest-run protoscience boot-strapped itself up into science.

Connecting the two heavenly ideas—solstice sightlines and eclipse forecasting—isn't obvious, or I'd be reading about this in an old book rather than running around looking puzzled. More facts often help generate more ideas, so I continued to examine the ancient Anasazi sites on the Colorado Plateau to get some inspiration from the ancient architects, to visit the Pueblos to get some ideas from the Anasazi's descendants.

CANYON VIEWS AND MESA-TOP VIEWS ARE VERY DIFferent. Canyons, with their elevated horizons all around, provide lots of notches to index the seasonal movements of the sun, enabling the Indians to create a seasonal calendar for planting and ceremonies. The mesa tops favored by most of the remaining pueblos instead offer long views, like those at Stonehenge. Was the Anasazi's attraction to mesa tops a defensive strategy like Herod's at Masada, or is it also wrapped up in their cosmology? At Chaco Canyon in northwestern New Mexico, one sees a collection of Anasazi "towns" that link mesa and canyon.

Chaco Canyon is a long, wide, and not particularly deep canyon that wanders along for more than 20 kilometers of the high plateau in northwest New Mexico. Dozens of Anasazi sites lie along the length of this canyon and its surrounding mesa tops. Chaco has the most elaborate set of Anasazi ruins that remain anywhere. They exhibit the fanciest architecture, the finest masonry style, and the most elaborate road system.

Archaeologists, contemplating what has been found at Chaco during the last century, speculate that it might have been used *only* as a ceremonial center. Very few burials have been found. Estimates of Chaco's population, based on the number of rooms and assuming the usual mortality rates, suggest that either a lot of burials are missing or Chaco was more like a modern-day resort town, with lots of rooms for seasonal visitors that are healthy enough to travel, but with few people living there year-round (and so a small cemetery).

I somehow doubt that Chaco was a summer resort: Cornfields needed tending during the warm months, and irrigation water needed to be delivered to the fields. But visits near the time of the winter solstice would not interfere with farming. Perhaps each visiting family helped to build a

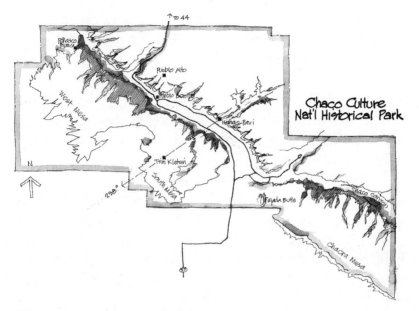

room onto 800-room Pueblo Bonito (another puzzle is that only several of the rooms show any sign of habitation via debris embedded in the floor).

Chaco is located about a hundred kilometers south of Mesa Verde, and some of Chaco's major roads lead north. But Chaco's prime was centuries before Mesa Verde's: its period of major construction was from about A.D. 900 until 1120. A few later structures were built in the Mesa Verde masonry style, so Chaco may have become an outpost of the Mesa Verde culture in the several centuries after the Chaco culture itself declined.

Yet Chaco's best centuries are among the most interesting, as the great expansion of Anasazi sites occurs about 1050 to 1100. In terms of widespread numbers and fancy architecture, the 900-1120 period may represent the height of the Anasazi culture, with Mesa Verde and Betatakin belonging to a later period just before the big decline. Chaco is not a canyon of cliff-dwellings, as there are few natural alcoves in its cliffy walls. While there are indeed a few cliff-dwellings, most of the ruins are situated out on the main floor of the canyon, separated somewhat from the cliffs in a manner quite unlike the more familiar Anasazi sites.

CHACO DID NOT SEEM LIKE A GOOD PLACE FOR studying the views from cliff-dwelling alcoves, but it has a lot of kivas, including some huge "Great Kivas" that antedate many of the small kivas that one sees at Chaco and elsewhere. So I eventually got around to visiting Chaco—and at the winter solstice. A picture of a sunrise in the right place is worth far more than any set of calculations based on magnetic compass readings.

"All roads lead to Chaco" might have been an Anasazi slogan, though the modern driver cursing the heavily rutted dirt roads might have other thoughts in mind after several hours of approaching Chaco Culture National Historical Park. I doubt that the Anasazi's roads ever became rutted and washboarded, because the prehistoric Indians had no wheeled vehicles. No horses, either.

So whatever did they need roads for? I have an anthropologist friend, Astrida Blukis Onat, who thinks that the answer to the road puzzle is foot races, the barefooted runners having some incentive to clear a racecourse. Long before marathon madness swept the Western world, foot races were popular among Indians of the Southwest. An annual race from Taos Pueblo to Grand Canyon, nearly 800 kilometers (500 miles), has been run in recent years.

Walking around Pueblo Alto on the top of North Mesa, I had some difficulty in seeing the ancient road from Mesa Verde. But the multispectral scanning techniques that supplement aerial photographs have shown a wide network of roads, all converging on Chaco. On the ground, the best way to spot an ancient road is to look for a suspiciously straight swath of sagebrush; the old roadbed probably channels rainwater, and so the plants grow better.

And if you think that modern road-builders have a passion for building straight roads that ignore natural obstacles, just go look and see what happened to the road south from Mesa Verde to Chaco, once it ran out of mesa and reached the edge of Chaco Canyon. The Jackson Staircase is a series of steps carved into the sandstone cliff, wide enough for a procession to continue over the top of the cliff and down its steep face. No switchbacks. The Chaco builders started carving an even wider flight of steps nearby, but never finished the job. Stepping down the cliff face, I suppose, might have been the finish of a foot race—but it seems likely that their roads also had some ceremonial purpose, probably linked to their religious cosmology.

EVENING WAS COMING AT CHACO WHEN I HIKED BACK to the trailhead, but there was about a half-hour to go before sunset. I drove quickly down to the first major town, Hungo Pavi, and hiked quickly out to its kiva.

I watched the sun set over the opposite wall of Chaco Canyon, a totally undistinguished section of horizon. There was nothing even remotely cornerlike, no notches, no peaks except for a tree that probably was not there a millennium ago. So much, I thought, for Chaco—it's going to be as bad as Mesa Verde.

But in the southeast, a distant cliff rose up like a headland, forming a distinct step from the distant canyon floor. My compass suggested that the top of that cliff was on the sun's path—might it, I wondered, function in the manner of that sunrise step at Perfect Kiva? Standing elsewhere in the ruined town didn't seem anywhere as promising; the angles changed so that the cliff was no longer on the sun's path through the sky. Tomorrow morning, I promised myself, I would be here with a camera rather than a compass, if only those clouds in the western sky did not move in and spoil things.

THE MORNING OF WINTER SOLSTICE, I AWOKE AN hour before the time I'd calculated the sun would rise over the top of that cliff. I drove up to Hungo Pavi with time to spare, and sat in the car keeping warm until the sunrise hit the far walls of the canyon. Then I bundled up and headed down the trail with my camera and little tape recorder. I was, of course, the only person anywhere. What a way, I mused, to celebrate the winter solstice. I doubted that it was as quiet in the pueblos.

Clouds in the southeastern sky promised rain, but the sky behind my cliff was clear, to my considerable relief. I waited, looking at the top of that distant southeastern cliff for the first signs of the sunrise. But it seemed, judging from the brightening of the sky, as if my compass bearing had been wrong. The sun was going to rise minutes earlier than predicted—and from the bottom of the cliff, not its top! Something had been wrong with my compass, I realized (Chaco Canyon, I later noticed, has iron nodules embedded in the sandstone cliffs, causing magnetic reading errors of several degrees in many places).

When the first gleam of the sun finally appeared, it was indeed in that bottom corner, where the vertical cliff edge intersected the horizontal stretch of distant horizon. It slowly rose to fill the frame: when its bottom touched the horizon, its left edge was touching the cliff wall. The sun had been "cornered," once again!

As I had suspected, there wasn't much choice in where to stand at Hungo Pavi; if I stood at any of the other major parts of the "town," the sun wouldn't fit into the corner. The kiva was again in the right place.

Back in the car with the heater running full blast again, I finished dictating my notes. Then I sat back and began to think about these special views that I was seeing from kivas: so far, they were always winter solstice views, either of sunrise or sunset, always with the sun framed in a corner, either formed by an alcove overhang or just a corner feature of a more distant cliff. It wasn't positioning the sun behind a peak or a notch of some sort, the way that the known features of the Hopi's horizon calendar functioned.

Still, I had the chance problem to overcome, the one that had bothered me so much at Betatakin. While there was some consistency—the favored directions were always winter solstice—what I really needed to beat the percentages was a second solstice sightline that intersected in the same kiva. I needed more double plays, as in Anasazi Valley.

It's too bad that Hungo Pavi doesn't have a winter solstice sunset view, I mused. I looked again at that feature-less horizon to the southwest. I tried out the pocket transit and binoculars again, but there just wasn't anything up there except some low trees. The canyon rim was as featureless and bland as the one seen from the Mesa Verde cliff dwellings. Perhaps I should hike up to the top of South Mesa and walk along that horizon one sees from the Hungo Pavi kiva? Try backsighting, just as I did at Mesa Verde, and find the right place for a cliff-edge shrine?

THE TOPOGRAPHIC MAP WAS LAID OUT ON THE HOOD of the car, its corners held down against the wind by flash-lights and cameras. I wanted to draw a line from the Hungo Pavi kiva to the sunset on the winter solstice. Since the horizon was elevated about 3° as seen from the kiva, my computer said that the right direction was *238°*. I penciled in a straight line from the kiva to the mesa at *238°*. But I drew the line a little too long, continuing it back across the top of the mesa.

The line ran into something—a ruin up atop South Mesa, called Tsin Kletzin by the Navajo. It's quite a way back from what looks to be the edge of the mesa top, but maybe. . . . Maybe the Sun Priest standing at Hungo Pavi's kiva could have seen Tsin Kletzin in the old days, maybe it poked up into the skyline to form a marker for the winter sunset seen from Hungo Pavi. That might provide two inter-secting sightlines at the kiva, and get me down to only a one-in-a-thousand chance of being fooled by a mere coincidence.

I hiked up that trail to Tsin Kletzin a lot faster than my usual snail's pace. Could I see Hungo Pavi from standing up at Tsin Kletzin? The topographic map said no, a near miss of less than about one-third of a degree, but maps have been wrong before. Seeing was believing. If I could see backward from Tsin Kletzin to Hungo Pavi, then surely the priest could see Tsin Kletzin from down below at the kiva, in the old days when Tsin Kletzin stuck up higher on the skyline.

Once atop South Mesa, Tsin Kletzin stands in the distance, almost a mound in a flat field of scrub brush. As I walked toward it, I could see nothing of Chaco Canyon, only North Mesa which lay beyond the canyon. The disappearing canyon. Tsin Kletzin was set back far from the edge of the mesa, not close to anything, out in the middle of nowhere. It's an enigmatic place, and not at all a site that had been used and reused. All of the trees used in its construction were cut in the three years starting in A.D. 1111 (known via the wonders of tree-ring dating), so it was a century or two younger than Hungo Pavi and most other ruins on the canyon floor. It was one of the last towns built before the droughts associated with Chaco's decline.

Tsin Kletzin is unusual in having several "tower kivas." They are not towering anymore, but the archaeologists can estimate their former height from the thickness of the walls, comparing them with the tower kivas that remain standing at other sites (such as Kin Klizhin, some miles south of Chaco proper). When the Anasazi built a four-story masonry wall, they started with a thick wall at the base and made it thinner as it ascended. And the Tsin Kletzin kivas have thick foundations, suggesting a few stories' height.

When I climbed up atop the ruins of Tsin Kletzin, I could barely see the canyon walls of Chaco, descending into that distant groove in the landscape. Even at the highest point of the ruins, I could see only about half of the depth of Chaco Canyon. I certainly couldn't see Hungo Pavi near the floor of the canyon. But what if the tower kiva were still standing, could I have seen Hungo Pavi from its top?

That evening, after having watched the sun set over the mesa, I measured the elevations carefully from the topographic map and did a little trigonometry. The horizon elevation from Hungo Pavi should be 2.95°, very close to the 3.0° I'd measured with the pocket transit several times. How far would the tower kiva have to stick up to show above that horizon? If it (or a projecting "flagpole") rose several stories further than present (24 feet or 7 meters), it would form an excellent corner of skyline in which the sun would seem to set when viewed from the Hungo Pavi kiva.

Furthermore, there were two tower kivas up there. As best I can tell from the archaeological map of the site, the second one would have stood alongside the first when viewed along that sightline from Hungo Pavi, rather like those Stonehenge stones framing a narrow sightline. The slot between the two tower kivas looks like good old *238°* again, the sightline up from the Hungo Pavi kiva to winter solstice sunset.

Had the Anasazi built a whole town, just to create a corner or a slot? Maybe. The direction from Hungo Pavi's kiva is exactly the right one for marking the winter solstice sunset. But why hadn't the Anasazi built Tsin Kletzin on the edge of the mesa, in plain view of Hungo Pavi? Why is it set back by 670 meters, so that an extra-tall tower kiva was needed to compensate? Could that middle-of-the-mesa spot be the intersection of two sightlines, so that the towers were doing double duty? I tried all of the known ruins in the area, to see if Tsin Kletzin was in a solstice or equinox direction from any of them. No luck, though it is possible that it would have been a summer solstice sunset view from some ruins farther down Chaco Canyon outside the park boundaries. Archaeologists prospecting for new ruins might want to look along solstice sightlines to and from Tsin Kletzin.

The Tsin Kletzin towers in Hungo Pavi's sunset might, of course, simply be a consequence of a town plan that favored cardinal directions for orienting structures. Washington, D.C., serves as an example: If you stand at the Capitol building, the Washington Monument is due west—and so at the equinoxes, the sun nestles into the corner that the spire forms with the horizon. That's a consequence of the town plan's fondness for cardinal directions. Another consequence are the curses of the rush-hour motorist near the equinoxes

when sunset occurs directly at the end of an east-west street, framed by buildings on either side, the setting sun shining right in the motorist's eyes. A town plan that avoided street orientations within the sunset possibilities (about *240-300°* at such latitudes) would circumvent that hazard, e.g., simply rotate the usual square street grid about 45° from the usual north-east-south-west.

THINKING OF TOWER KIVAS AS INDEX FEATURES RE-minded me of the downstep at Perfect Kiva, and of how one could pivot about it, maintaining a standard view from day to day, the observer's position becoming the measurement. Was a tower kiva at Tsin Kletzin situated away from the edge of the cliff so that priests could walk around it in a circle, a good distance away? This thought served to remind me of that sidestepping scheme for Perfect Kiva.

To make the sidestepping method work atop a mesa with a tower kiva merely requires that you adopt a standard criterion for the rising sun. For example, to keep the rising sun nestled into the corner formed by the horizon and the tower, you will need to stand in a different place tomorrow than you did today. Near the equinoxes, the sun's position on the horizon changes by more than a diameter from one day to the next; with a 600-meter radius, that means that the ob-server would be as many as seven or eight paces away from the previous day's observing position. That's hard to miss noticing. The differences would diminish as the solstice neared, little sidesteps merging into a standstill lasting for days and days, then turning around.

Of course, you do not need to build a tower kiva to get a corner—any cliff around here will do, at least for some of the year. Move around from day to day, keeping that standard view of the sun nestled between the horizon and the rising cliff face, looking like that Hungo Pavi solstice sunrise view. The advantage of a tower atop a flat mesa is that the same corner can be used all year, for both sunrise and sunset measurements. That offset of Tsin Kletzin from the canyon rim would have been handy for making sunset measurements on the days when sunrise was clouded.

EQUINOX IS HALFWAY ALONG THE ARC BETWEEN WINTER and summer solstice viewing positions. But maybe the Anasazi didn't think in terms of bisecting angles (which can be simply done via stretching out a rope between the extreme positions and then folding it in half). If they were counting consistently, you might suppose that they could count the days between solstices and divide by two. But you would be wrong; because the earth speeds up in its orbit when closer to the sun, the "quarter-years" are of unequal length, ranging from 91 to 94 days (91 days from winter solstice to spring equinox, which is why February has only 28 days). What simpler way might they have had of locating the equinoxes?

The Two Priests method for warning of lunar eclipses can also be used to find the equinox day. No index is needed. Just stand out on the mesa top somewhere with a clear view of eastern and western horizons.

We tend to speak of the equinoxes as when the days and nights are of equal length, patently an impossible determination before clocks. But the equinox is also when the sunrise and sunset lie along a straight line that includes the observer. At winter solstice in Chaco, the sun rises at $120°$ from due north and sets at $240°$; that's a 120° dogleg angle between them. At summer solstice, sunrise has moved northeast to $60°$, the sunset to $300°$, opening up that acute dogleg angle into a hyperextended oblique angle. Midway through the cycle, sunrise and sunset lie along a straight line from $90°$ to $270°$. Given how much the angle changes from day to day near the midpoint of the cycle, you're going to have one

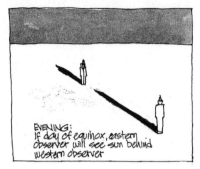

day when it's almost 180° from sunrise to sunset, and the next day it will be a little more than 180°.

But how would an Anasazi have measured this straight line, given that the measurements have to be separated in time by 12 hours? In the morning, the two priests play the initial part of their game: *A* stands still at a spot marked on the ground and *B* moves around until the sunrise is just behind *A*. He marks the spot. Just before sunset, the two priests return and take up the positions they had marked on the ground that morning. It is now *A*'s turn to watch, without moving off his marker, and see if the sunset occurs exactly behind *B*. The day before the equinox, sunset will be just to one side of *B*. The next night, it will be immediately behind *B* or just a little to the other side. That's the equinox.

Did they actually do this? The Chaco Anasazi do seem to have known about the east-west line associated with the equinox. At Pueblo Alto, atop North Mesa where the road comes south from Mesa Verde, a long east-west wall extends through the entire town. And the great kiva, Casa Rinconada, has a perfect north-south axis (and there was no Pole Star back then) with niches along the east-west line. The eastern Pueblos indeed use north-east-south-west as their cardinal directions today, but this may be due to European influence; certainly the Hopi and Zuni, the least influenced of all the Pueblos, use solstice directions.

You can't use the Two Priests method, for either equinox determination or eclipse warning, down in a canyon because the elevated horizons will interfere. But a few diameters of horizon elevation total (either in the east or the west, or some in each) won't cause serious errors. Indeed, by offsetting the bending of light rays by the atmosphere, the slightly elevated horizons will help the observers make the measurement near the true horizontal. The east and west views from Pueblo Alto total about 3-4 diameters of horizon elevation; if they used the first gleam of sunrise and the last gleam of sunset, they should have been able to determine the equinox to within a day of what modern techniques give. And the long uplands are not the only mesas that could be used; the truncated mountains such as Acoma's mesa, or the peninsula such as Cape Royal would function nicely for equinox determination, especially if the criterion of the sun sitting atop the horizon were used.

The equinox would make a good New Year's Day, instead of the New Year's Day we use, just ten days after the winter solstice. Because the sunrise or sunset position moves $0.6°$ every day in the spring and autumn, you can get a clear yes-or-no answer to the question: Has spring started yet? Nothing dramatic may happen to the sun on that particular day, but if you're measuring, it is easy to tell before and after: The eastern observer sees the sunset move from one side of the western observer to the other, just from one day to the next.

IT WAS BEGINNING TO LOOK AS IF THE ANASAZI LIKED their solstice sun to rise and set in corners—so much so that they'd build a corner, if a natural one wasn't in the right place. And that they would use a variety of framing schemes. I felt that I was, at last, beginning to see things the way that the Anasazi did back in the American stone ages. They liked to corner the sun.

The Mayan glyph for sunrise was indeed a circle sitting atop a stone, with another stone framing one side of the circle at an acute angle to the base. There are a number of variations on the sunrise glyph, but in all of them the "sun" looks as if trapped in a funnel. Thus it seems possible that cornering the

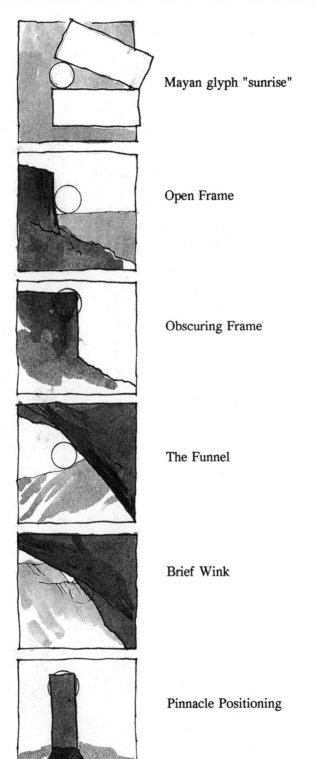

Mayan glyph "sunrise"

Open Frame

Obscuring Frame

The Funnel

Brief Wink

Pinnacle Positioning

sun was more widespread than just Anasazi. While Mayan influences are seen in Anasazi archaeology, they are relatively infrequent—at least, compared to what you see in the Anasazi's contemporaries just to the south, the Sinagua (who had ball courts and other characteristically Mayan architecture). More than parrots made the trip north.

So we are seeing a variety of cornering criteria at the various Anasazi sites:

- *The Funnel*, where the sun sets into an acute angle (or emerges from one);
- *The Open Frame*, where the entire sun is visible, sitting atop a horizon with one side against a framing cliff;
- *The Obscuring Frame*, where a downstep in a horizon frames the sun, and all but an edge or two is obscured (the solstice sunrise at Perfect Kiva that looks like a solar eclipse is perhaps the perfect example). Cliff tops would make good obscuring frames, as would pinnacles.
- *The Brief Wink*, where a flash occurs in a corner after the sun has otherwise set (or, I suppose, before the sun normally rises).

The open frames are indeed low in the sky (higher, and they would be impossible in practice due to the sun's brightness). The obscuring frames and late winks are all high, at elevations more like 12-15° off the horizontal. Frames are convenient because of "boxing in" the sun; if you only see one gleam of light and the horizon isn't horizontal (as with "The Funnel," those crescent corners in Anasazi Valley), you really don't know which portion of the sun's rim that you are seeing (that's the basic problem with emerging from a funnel-like angle).

I'm making progress—indeed, I have rediscovered some fine methods for detecting the equinox, and for keeping a day-by-day calendar throughout the year. But I still have no answers for the skeptic about *Exhibit B* (Of what use are solstice sightlines, if not for anchoring a calendar?) and *Exhibit A* (Why do we see artificial horizons that are elevated?). How do these observations all hang together? I was beginning to despair about connecting solstice sightlines to eclipse forecasting until I visited Canyon de Chelly.

8

Half a View
Provides the Clue

*We have lived upon this land from days beyond
history's records, far past any living memory, deep
into the time of legend. The story of my people and
the story of this place are one single story. No man
can think of us without thinking of this place. We
are always joined.*

A member of the Taos Pueblo

Hiking down to "paradise," it was difficult to maintain my preoccupation with why solstice sightlines were so common; the views are too distracting. I have no idea what the Anasazi's name for Canyon de Chelly was, but I'll bet that it was something like "paradise." About 30 stories deep, the canyon's clifflike walls are forbidding in most places. Unlike Chaco's half-mile-wide bottom, the flat bottomlands of Canyon de Chelly are only about a block or two wide. A creek flows along peacefully, and it is good farm country. This is a protected place, just the sort that novelists create, with hidden entrances that open from a desert into a garden paradise. Small wonder that the Navajo treasure it. Surely the Anasazi did.

Canyon de Chelly is west of Chaco, just over the Arizona border. Like Betatakin, it is now a national monument surrounded by the Navajo Indian Reservation. The Navajo are not Pueblo peoples, but they seem similar in many ways. Their agriculture, even their religion, has many elements in common with the Pueblos. The Navajo are even closer to hunting and gathering than the Pueblo peoples, having hunted and gathered their way down to the Southwest from the far north a mere 500 years ago. They, and the Apache to their south and the Utes in Colorado, are Athapaskan peoples, the linguists first having discovered these relationships from the similarity of their languages to those of the Indians of Alaska and Canada's Yukon Territory. Had Columbus discovered the New World a few centuries earlier, the conquistadors wouldn't have seen any "Apaches with cultivated fields" (that's said to be how the Navajo got their Spanish name).

The Navajo learned farming from the Pueblo peoples, and settled down to compete with them for territory. They are now far more numerous: 210,000 Navajo versus 50,000 Pueblo peoples. The Navajo even adopted many elements of the Pueblo religion which, once one understands how intertwined are the Pueblo agricultural practices with their religious customs, makes some sense. The Navajo have been a vigorous, adaptable people—but because of that, their hunter-gatherer Athapaskan culture has been waning.

This is what usually happens, and what makes the really conservative Pueblo peoples so important. Perhaps their close identification with their traditional surroundings makes them slow to adopt new ways or move to new places. The Pueblos may not be particularly representative of Anasazi-style ancestors—not any more than such highly conservative sects as the Amish are representative of European postindustrial civilization. Still, a composite guess about *any* neolithic American culture is infinitely better than what we know of the Stone Age people who built Stonehenge, which, outside of megaliths, toolmaking technology, and some population density estimates, is almost nothing.

THIS "PARADISE" IS SHAPED LIKE A WISHBONE. CANyon de Chelly has two arms, each extending about 20 miles; one runs northeast and the other southeast from their junction. Anasazi cliff-dwellings there are set back into great alcoves like those of Anasazi Valley and Betatakin.

White House Ruin is in the southeast branch. The hiking trail to it passes some unusual shapes eroded into the sandstone. One looks like a pair of eyeglasses, hollow sockets behind them. Smaller hollows have trapped blowing soil over the years, and then some seeds, and now bright green plants hang here and there along the reddish-brown cliffs.

Down and down the trail winds. Eventually one comes to a tunnel hewn out of the rock in recent decades, saving the visitor a somewhat perilous traverse along a cliff ledge that the Indians probably didn't mind very much.

White House Ruin is seen both on the valley floor of Canyon de Chelly and in the alcove a few stories above. The mesa top and the distant horizon form the top of the picture. The streaks of "desert varnish" are a common feature of red sandstones and limestones.

Emerging from the tunnel, you are amidst trees, and an unusual farmhouse lies ahead. It is a traditional Navajo hogan, a round one-room house, with a doorway facing east. I think that some novelist I've read must have been there before me—I had a strong sense of déjà vu as I came out of the tunnel into the sunny bottomlands.

The path continues through some sheltering cotton-wood trees, and then opens out onto the banks of the wide creek. Except where the creek narrows down, the water seems to be less than knee-deep. As you look up, the opposite canyon wall rises, and you see a large alcove containing many cliff-dwellings. Large streaks of black desert varnish lead down from the top of the cliff like paint-can drips, terminating all around the alcove, a magnificent sight.

Close up (and slightly wet), you see a series of rooms on the bottomland of the canyon, rooms that probably were flooded during a spring runoff. A few stories above them, requiring a ladder to reach, is the ground floor of the alcove,

143

facing south as a proper Anasazi alcove should. The Anasazi used ladders made out of thin tree trunks, cutting off branches in such a way as to leave enough for a step. The Park Service has prepared the lower rooms for the onslaught of visitors, but the upper stories are plainly intended to be permanently out of reach to non-Anasazi. The alcove seems a likely candidate for solstice corners, from somewhere in its depths, worth investigating with pocket transit—however, that's for another day.

The cottonwoods near the creek afforded shade in the summer; the alcove got the low winter sun much of the day. By Anasazi standards, there was a lot of water; they were likely the envy of their neighbors, which may explain why the access to the cliff-dwellings was not improved by cutting steps into the cliff face. When outlying marginal areas dried up and lost their corn crop, which happened every few decades in this land of fickle rainfall, those outlying people probably searched for a source of grain. Canyon de Chelly surely had water when most others didn't, and they were probably raided for food supplies. That's one disadvantage of living in paradise.

You can see high ledges near the top of some alcoves, big enough for birds to roost. But the birds' space seems to have been usurped by a few sealed pots of grain. They're hard to get to, probably requiring little-known steps and ladders hidden down the canyon somewhere, so most raiders never managed to get up there before being driven off. The hidden grain could serve as the backup supply for the inhabitants of paradise—and, even more importantly, serve as the essential seed corn, sure to be available at planting time next spring, no matter how hungry people got. Its inaccessibility was probably intended to keep out the local people in times of hunger, as well as any starving raiders.

I SETTLED DOWN IN THE SHADE OF THE COTTON-woods on the south side of the stream, with a view of the White House alcove across the way, complete with the long desert-varnish "drips" overhanging it. And I tried to work out the accumulated puzzles.

Anasazi astronomy seems, at first glimpse, to be a more detailed version of those archaeoastronomy findings from around the world: judging by how stones are aligned and where buildings are constructed, solstice directions were very popular. Yet agriculturally, nothing interesting happens in midwinter or midsummer. And even if it did, the sunrise position changes so slowly at the solstices that you'd get year-to-year fluctuations of a week or more (in the Pekwin story, 20 days!). Those Hopi conventions about intermediate sunrise positions for planting time are simplicity itself.

A different kind of usefulness, as Columbus made clear, is eclipse prediction. It can be a powerful technique for personal advancement (or saving one's neck); perhaps that is what's behind constructing solstice sightlines, not agricultural considerations? Yet none of the simple entry-level methods (nor, I might add, any of the known intermediate-level methods such as the 56-hole Stonehenge ones and the Mayan cycle) use solstices explicitly; the counting-by-sixes prediction doesn't even use sightlines at all. What's so handy about solstice sightlines to the eastern and western horizons? Surely there is a way to match up the usefulness of eclipse forecasting to the most common astronomical interest expressed by many prehistoric peoples.

MY LUNAR ECLIPSE WARNING METHODS SEEM TO RE-quire a reasonably horizontal western horizon and a reasonably horizontal eastern horizon. Opposite views, as it were. If you live on an island, you hike to the south end or the north end, and you will have a sea horizon in both directions, just as at the Temple of Poseidon. On a large continent such as North America, however, finding the proper horizon can take some effort—such as hiking to the tip of the Florida peninsula, or the Yucatan peninsula, or Baja California.

Puget Sound, with all its islands and peninsulas combined with long stretches of water, is potentially an exception—but I still had trouble finding a viewpoint with long stretches of water to northwest and southeast plus low horizons, from which to observe a lunar eclipse in early August. I only located one such spot on the map, Dungeness Spit in the Strait of Juan de Fuca, which required a ten-mile round-trip hike to get far enough out to clear the horizon obstructions. I found a second spot on Whidbey Island, to the north of Seattle, with a five-mile path over water, but its southeast horizon was a little too high. One could, I suppose, try the higher mountaintops, which, while lacking in shining streaks of water (and requiring camping there overnight), are otherwise acceptable for distant horizons. I kept thinking wistfully of the high mesas in Anasazi country, with their long views, or the plains of Kansas where opposite views are easy to find.

Most people live in places without easy access to nice views of the sort I've been thinking in terms of, with their opposite views. Alas. If only there were some eclipse-warning use of half a view, some way to use northeast-to-southeast sunrise views without any need for a view to the sunset. How does one adapt to half a horizon?

THEN I REMEMBERED WHAT FRED HOYLE HAD MEN-tioned in passing in his Stonehenge book: When a lunar eclipse is due, the sun rises that morning about as far north of due east as the full moon will rise that evening to the south of due east (or vice versa). The simple rule is: Equal angles from due east.

Hoyle's method is really a variation on the 180° methods, and depends on the sunrise and sunset being equally far from the east-west line each day. If the sun rises 20° north of due east, i.e., at *70°* from north, then it will set about 20° north of due west that evening (*290°;* within 0.5°, at least). That means that the conical shadow will rise 20° south of due east, right? At *110°* from north? So that's the eclipse-prone position for a moonrise.

But how did they know where due east is located? De-

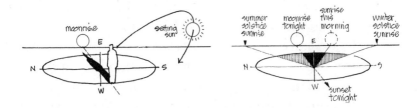

termining the equinox is possible using Two Priests, but it still seems a bit of a leap, given that the Anasazi's favorite directions emphasized the solstices rather than our north-east-south-west cardinal directions at *0°-90°-180°-270°*. So a method using due east is surely not a primary discovery but rather something intermediate, after the virtues of a right-angle coordinate system were discovered.

Then I tried Hoyle's method, but used the Pueblo's *60°-120°* solstice sunrise directions instead of due east at *90°*. Suppose, for example, that they measured the *70°* sunrise in mid–May as just 10° from the nearest solstice direction, i.e., the one at *60°*. The sun would set 10° south of the *300°* solstice direction at *290°*, which would make its conical shadow 10° north of the winter solstice sunrise line at *120°*. And indeed *110°* is the eclipse-prone position of moonrise. Hoyle's method works with the Anasazi's coordinate system as well as ours! The simple rule is: *If moonrise tonight is as far from the nearest solstice sightline as sunrise this morning was from the other solstice, watch out for an eclipse.*

COMPARING TWO ARCS, HOWEVER, SEEMS VERY DIFFER-ent from the other methods; this eastern-horizon-only method isn't entry-level, something that a prehistoric priest might have stumbled into. It is more complicated because you have to compare the sunrise's "distance" from a solstice sightline—a difference in sightlines, if you like—to what you see that evening at moonrise, discern if the full moon is the same "distance" from the other easterly solstice sightline. Such a method isn't really like measurement with a ruler, where you count your way along a graded scale; instead, it involves rendering a same-or-different judgment.

I doubt that the Anasazi needed any abstract notion of arcs and angles (the way that we teach geometry) in order to use this half-a-horizon method. Because the Anasazi were so fond of beaded necklaces, I imagine them holding the necklace at arm's length in the morning, with one end at the solstice sightline, finding the bead that was under the sunrise and then sliding the remaining beads away from this "sunrise bead," perhaps tying a knot there. And then that same evening, they would hold up the necklace to the moonrise and see if the full moon came close to the sunrise bead when the necklace's end was aligned with the other solstice sightline. Call it Method #7 ("The Arm's-Length Necklace").

We've solved the lunar eclipse warning problem for those folks living on an eastern coastline, having a sea horizon but only to the east. What about those poor folks inland, with an even horizon that is, alas, elevated several degrees? *It will still work*, surprisingly enough: those terrible problems with the 180° methods when horizons are elevated (changing a straight line into a dogleg) are minor when dealing with only an eastern horizon. Both sunrise and moonrise are

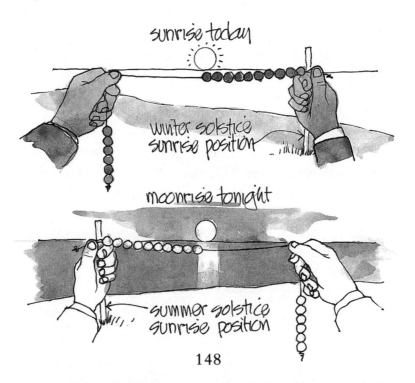

shifted south, but by nearly equal amounts. Since you're always comparing sunrise and moonrise directions with the solstice directions (also shifted), the errors cancel if the horizon between solstice sightlines remains equally elevated.

EUREKA MIGHT NOW SEEM AN APPROPRIATE EXCLAMAtion. Solstice directions are *very* useful because their sightlines serve as reference directions, allowing the use of the lunar eclipse warning methods on a northeast-to-southeast horizon, without any requirement about what's seen in the west. *Exhibit B,* explained?

And that may solve, in the same stroke, the puzzle of the elevated banks at the British megalithic monuments, what I called *Exhibit A.* The mildly elevated horizon isn't a complication anymore—just as long as it is *uniformly* elevated above a true horizontal (at least, in that one-sixth of the circle that you need, bracketing due east). You can take a bumpy horizon and flatten it out, just by building a level bank to obscure the bumps, across which you view sunrise and moonrise. They'll be shifted south a little, but so what? You establish the solstice directions in the presence of the elevated bank. Then you use those solstice sightlines at the full moon each month, to compare moonrise and sunrise positions.

I WAS HAPPILY PLAYING IN THE SAND ALONGSIDE THE creek when some hikers walked by. They probably thought that I was a little old to be building sand castles—and certainly out of practice. After all, the moat is the last thing that one builds, after the central structures. But I was building only an elevated bank, with no castle. The easy construction technique for a bank is to dig a ditch and pile the sand along one side of it. The water table being what it is in the creek bed, my ditch slowly filled up with water. But what's important for eclipse forecasting is that elevated bank.

But the moat is not merely a by-product: it is *very* useful, as it provides an easy way to level the top of the bank. The water is horizontal, so long as no one is making waves. Just

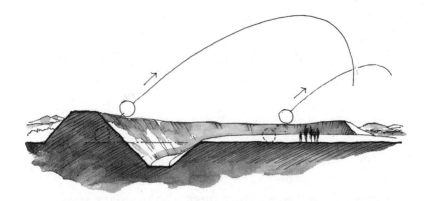

take a stick with a side branch remaining, and smooth the sand atop the bank while keeping the bottom of the stick at exactly the water line. That way, the top of the bank will be almost as level as the water's surface. For an observer near the center of the circle, it's a uniformly elevated horizon. At Avebury and Stonehenge, the winter rains probably filled the ditches that they dug into the underlying chalk. And all that floating chalk debris probably left behind one of the world's more obvious bathtub rings, allowing year-round construction to reference the high water line. A tree trunk with a side branch could be used to scale up my sand castle technique to flatten the top of the bank.

Pivoting around a corner-producing post or tower also ought to work well with an elevated bank. The pivot could be outside the bank, something like the Heel Stone at Stonehenge. Or the pivot could be inside the circular bank, though the accuracy would suffer unless you had a very big circle. So long as the pivot stuck up above the bank, as seen from the observer's path inside, you could track sunrise and moonrise, and compare them via the distances along the arc. At the south end of the observer's arc is the position for seeing summer solstice sunrise aligned on the pivot. At the north end, the winter solstice sunrise would look exactly the same, in the corner of the post or tower.

To measure the two arcs—no, it is *comparing*, not measuring—to compare the moonrise's distance from the

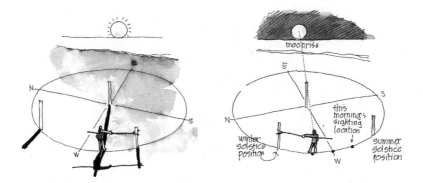

nearest solstice with what sunrise did that morning, I'd suggest using extra-long necklaces, the kind that can be looped
around your neck a dozen times. Stretch the necklace out
from the sunrise viewing position to the nearest solstice
sightline, then pick it up and carry it over to the other
solstice, stretch it out to predict the moonrise position.

A long stick would also suffice, held with one end
against a post at the nearer solstice sightline: *just walk over to
touch the stick to the other solstice post while holding the stick in the
same place, and you will be at the observation position at which an
about-to-be-eclipsed full moon will rise tonight in the pivot corner.*
The size of the stick, or length of the necklace, depends on
the distance from pivot to observer's path. The longer it is,
the more accurate you'll be. Call it Method #8 ("The Stick").

A UNIFORMLY ELEVATED HORIZON IS WHAT ALLOWS
those eclipse prediction methods to function in almost any
locale—though canyons might be an exception if you're
fussy about success rate. Sites with 15°-high features on the
horizon are not so promising, but I can imagine the 3° horizons at many locations in Chaco's central valley as eligible for
smoothing with a bank like Avebury's or Stonehenge's. I
haven't seen any such banks around there, however, and
filling the adjacent ditches with water might have been
harder in the desert than in England. Perhaps, I mused, there
is another way to elevate the horizon and level it.

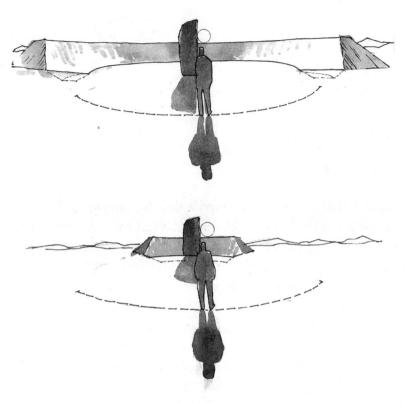

HOW LONG DOES THE LEVEL BANK NEED TO BE? I'D
sure want to make it as short as possible, if I were doing the
digging. The closer the horizontal edge is to the vertical
pivot that completes the corner, the less lengthy the bank can
be. If the Heel Stone were the pivot at Stonehenge, and they
had put that bank just inside it, the bank would only have
needed to be a few paces long.

In fact, why not just make the artificial horizon *at* the
pivot, as in those Framing the Sun examples where the horizontal aspect stayed constant: *Use Framing the Sun, but also
frame the moon and compare the observer distances from the nearest
solstice sightline!* Just have the observer maneuver until the
rising sun (or moon) is sitting atop the horizontal but with
one side against a vertical. Or, if the sun is too high in the sky
to look at, the observer obscures the sun behind the pivot so
that a slight gleam is seen at the top and another at the side.

So long as the observer's path is level (and many an old lake bed is quite flat), the edge of a cliff top will suffice as a frame (as long as it is higher than all the other horizon features that the observer sees while walking along his semiannual path).

Simplicity—no bank and ditch are needed, merely a pivot point that is shaped such that you can hide the sun behind it. Your observation path could be a circular arc around the pivot point (actually, a straight line running north-south will work almost as well). Remember that you aren't measuring per se, just comparing one arc with another (in post-Euclidean terms, you compare chords rather than arcs). Method #9 ("Pivot About the Frame") is a very forgiving method.

THANKS TO THE PREOCCUPATION OF NEW WORLD AR-chaeoastronomers with windows, and the Old World archae-oastronomers with pivots, I realized that there is a homely substitute for bank-and-ditch. The Navajo hogan just up-stream from the cliff-dwellings reminded me of it, what with its east-facing doorway. A level floor can, in effect, substitute for a level horizon, so long as there is an east-facing window or door.

I don't have much experience living in hogans, so I'll explain this method using my bedroom back in Seattle. My bed faces east, and there is a small window high on the eastern wall. In the summer, when the sun rises in the north-east, its first rays come in through the window obliquely and strike the southwest corner of the room. There's a nice rose-colored patch of light, the shape of the eastern window. A half hour later, the shadow line of the window frame has moved down the western wall toward my bed, swinging both to the north and downward as the sun swings south and up (the window frame acts as a pivot).

Suppose that on the summer solstice, we mark the floor, denoting where the shadow corner intersects the floor. We do the same at winter solstice. Then on various mornings

throughout the year, we can lay out a necklace (or belt, or stick) along the floor from sunrise to nearest solstice, and move it over to the other solstice mark in order to predict the eclipse-prone position of the full moon that same evening.

The same thing will happen in most Navajo hogans. The shadow line of the upper south corner of the east-wall door frame will sweep down the back wall of the hogan until it finally reaches the floor. Personally, were I trying to use a doorway, I'd create a little window atop the lintel by omitting some mud mortar—something like that hole drilled above the doorway in the square cave at Tsankawi—and use that little spot of light against the back wall rather than the door frame's shadow. The hogan, being round, makes the method analogous to those circular pivot paths. But you could also do it with a west wall that ran north-south (you're only comparing, not measuring), such as in my Seattle bedroom.

The pueblo people are known to use crystals inside kivas to reflect the light that shines through the entryway; placing a crystal at the eclipse-prone position along the arc might serve to reflect moonlight around the kiva, creating an eclipse warning visible to all. Several crystals either side of the dangerous position (a rhinestone belt comes to mind) would help accurately measure the umbra-penumbra boundary; the first crystal to glow as the shadow edge descends would serve to mark the spot. Though star-watching has been mentioned to the Pueblo historians, I don't know of any evidence for seasonal sun-watching from within kivas in the historic pueblos. Traditional Pueblo secrecy, of course, makes the aphorism "Absence of evidence is not evidence of absence" particularly cautionary.

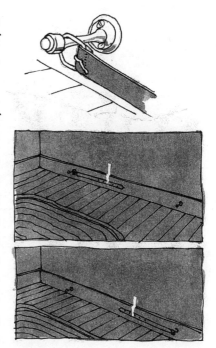

So an east-facing window is all it takes to warn of eclipses? The more you know, the simpler it gets. That horizontal floor (or level shelf, or kiva-like bench) serves as the elevated horizon here—the pivot around the door's lintel just inverted it, and the angle of elevation is the angle between floor line and door top (it needs to be greater than the highest feature along the eastern horizon, but ought not be much greater).

Method #10 ("The Hogan") is only as accurate as the room is large. Those great kivas at Chaco would have allowed far more accuracy than the typical kiva or hogan or Seattle bedroom (though there are some limits, from smearing out the shadow edges). When the method is used in a small room, it might be so inaccurate as to be worthless for eclipse prediction. Still, like the small sundials, it might have proven popular nonetheless—and, come to think of it, the great kivas are dated earlier than the small ones.

PINNACLES ABOUND IN CANYON DE CHELLY. THE most spectacular is Spider Rock. Pinnacles (and, I realized, similar constructions such as tower kivas) provide another way of elevating the horizon. When the sun is rising, you stand far enough away so that a little sun peeks around both left and right sides of the tower. As the sun rises further, you'll have to move left repeatedly. Eventually the sun will

155

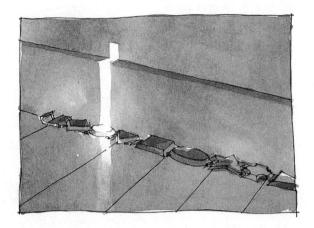

peek over the top as well (a three-point obscuring frame!) and it will become too bright to look at.

You'll have to look away, perhaps look down at your feet—at the position where you've come to stand, after all of that sidestepping. Because you stand at the right distance to see both left and right edges of the sun, your semiannual path will be rounded, about one-sixth of an imaginary circle about the pinnacle. If this viewing path is on fairly level ground, you're all set to warn of eclipses via viewing moonrise the same way, comparing distances from the adjacent solstices.

Now that might be the way to find any precision pivoting pathways left by the Anasazi. Stand far enough west of a candidate pinnacle to obscure the morning sun except for a gleam at both left and right. Then look around the nearby mesa, to see if you are standing along some sort of circular segment, perhaps overgrown with sagebrush as were those Anasazi roads leading to Chaco Canyon. Do-it-yourselfers can always use a local utility pole to similarly mask the sun: Method #11 is "The Pinnacle Pivot's Pathway."

The broader the pivot, the farther away you have to stand—and consequently, the longer are the distances be-

tween sunrise observing positions from one day to the
next. Because the three-point
frame for the sun is so reliable
(you stop moving when the
first gleam of sun is seen over
the top), great accuracy can

priest marks today's position — *yesterday's*

be achieved. As long as the pinnacle's top is the same height
when seen from the southwest as from the northwest (such as
a round tower or a utility pole with a flat top), and so long as
the observer's arc is reasonably level (old lake beds would be
ideal), reliability should be excellent—and it's certainly easier
to construct!

Actually, pinnacles aren't essential for either calendar or
eclipse uses. Any cliff profile or building edge will suffice
(you keep *one* edge of the sun or moon in sight until it crests).
Nor is a circular path essential for eclipse warning: a straight-
line path that is approximately north-south will do (and for
calendar-only use, even that requirement can be relaxed).

Will a view of only the western horizon suffice? For a
calendar, certainly—but not for lunar eclipse prediction (the
eclipse would already be over by the time you measured
moonset!). Creating a good calendar is even easier than forecasting eclipses, thanks to the "mechanical advantage" of
light levers.

WHEN I HIKED BACK UP THE TRAIL OUT OF CANYON
de Chelly, a thunderstorm swept over the area. Fortunately,
I'd just passed a small cave in the cliff alongside the trail, so I
ran back down to it. No larger than a park bench, it accom-
modated me nicely. I looked out on Canyon de Chelly, seeing
the thunderstorm pass over. The view was limited to a small
patch of canyon, that being one problem with alcoves, so I
did not see the rainbow until I emerged from the shelter.

I wondered what the view would have been like from up
in the White House Ruin, what living in such a place would
have done to shape your view of the world around you. It

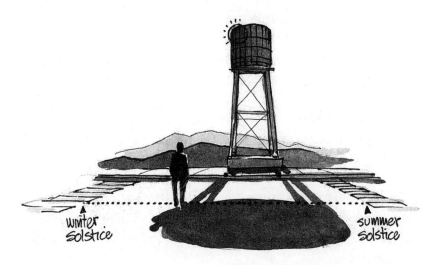

winter
solstice

summer
solstice

certainly provided many opportunities to learn about how
the sun moves through the sky with the changing seasons,
and how the moon almost mimics the sun's movements on a
far faster time scale. You would have been surrounded by
natural measuring instruments, available for forecasting
eclipses, thereby improving your chances of stumbling onto
one of the simple methods, quite without intending to do so.

9

When Sunrise Is an Illuminated Eye: Winter Solstice Seen from the Bottom of the Grand Canyon

Most of the Soyal rites [winter solstice ceremonies at Hopi] take place in the kiva. One of the most significant occurs on the evening of the ninth day and consists in a dancer depicting the hesitant course of the sun returning toward the summer solstice . . . At Walpi a group of Singers forces the carrier of a shield in the form of a sun to return to the correct road.

the ethnologist ARLETTE FRIGOUT, *1979*

From the Hopi's Third Mesa, you look west and see the Grand Canyon on the horizon—at least, on a clear day. A sulphurous haze is becoming common, thanks to the smokestacks of the giant coal-burning power plant just north of the Hopi Reservation.

South of Third Mesa, you can see the canyon of the Little Colorado River making its way northwest toward the Grand Canyon. A few miles before the confluence of the Little Colorado with the Colorado River inside Grand Canyon is a hot springs dome to which the Hopi trace their origins. In Hopi cosmology, people emerged from the underworld through that very "sipapu" and the dead return to the underworld through it (there is a symbolic sipapu—a hole in the floor—in every kiva). Shrines are located all along the route from the Hopi villages to the Grand Canyon, where the final shrine is located in some small alcoves on the banks of the Colorado River. Undertaking a journey to visit these places can be part of growing up Hopi.

Just around the corner, as it were, from that final shrine in the Grand Canyon are Anasazi agricultural sites. The canyon opens out into bottomlands for a dozen miles on both sides of the river, finally narrowing again just below Unkar Delta. Has the Pueblo tradition forgotten this part of their Anasazi heritage (which seems to date from about A.D. 700 to about 1100)? Or do they merely avoid mentioning them to outsiders? If they visit farther downriver than Mile 64, the Hopi certainly don't leave behind prayer sticks and other offerings.

I was particularly curious about that Cardenas Hilltop Ruin at Mile 71, across the river from Unkar Delta where I saw the lunar eclipse. The view from there provided a wonderful horizon calendar because of all those notches in the eastern rim of the Grand Canyon. When I had projected some color slides at home, which had been taken at my request from that hilltop by Larry Stevens, an ecologist working nearby, I noticed that the southeast skyline had a hole in it, through which you could see blue sky. That turned out to be where my calculations said that winter solstice sunrise ought to be: shining through the hole in the wall. But I couldn't be precise about where you stood to see it. It was surely someplace along that southwest ridgeline on the Cardenas hilltop. Was the ruin the "Right Spot" to stand? I couldn't be sure, just from the map. But the map is not the territory; I'd just have to consult the territory.

And, of course, I couldn't resist going to see the winter solstice sunrise from the ruin—with a little help from my friends.

THE CARDENAS SOLSTICE EXPEDITION EVENTUALLY IN-volved seven of us who hiked down to observe the solstice sunrise. We assembled at Lipan Point on the South Rim of Grand Canyon, which often has a clear view of the Colorado River in the region where the canyon bottom opens out. You can see the river make a U-turn around a hill: that's Cardenas, all of about 40 stories above the river. With binoculars, the hilltop ruin is visible at the juncture of several ridgelines. On the far side of the river is Unkar Delta, probably the winter home of the Anasazi who lived on the North Rim.

Lipan Point is where the trail starts, dropping down into the Grand Canyon. It was snowing lightly as we started out, but it was the old ice on various sections of the trail that caused us to be cautious. Robert Euler, the Park Service anthropologist at the Grand Canyon, was the only one of us who had the foresight to bring along instep crampons, handy for such icy patches. Bob went along with us just for part of the first day, returning to his South Rim office to remain in radio contact with us; he's the expert on Cardenas Ruin, having dated the pottery fragments found near it to about A.D. 1100. My wife, Katherine Graubard, stayed on the rim and ran the radios for the five days of the expedition, keeping us supplied with weather forecasts.

Hiking down, Bob explained that the Paleo-Indians were in the canyon for many millennia before the Anasazi, that some caves were sites where they left split-twig figurines, presumably as offerings. A willow branch is split for most of its length, then folded into the shape of an animal, the willow ends tucked in to create the appearance of a spear embedded in the animal. Some are dated to 4,000 years ago.

We camped halfway down the trail, far enough down in altitude to be rid of the ice but still likely to be snowed upon during the night. Our camp was not far from an old Anasazi campsite, judging from all the pottery fragments that Bob Euler had analyzed from this hilltop. We enjoyed a wonderful sunset view—not only of the Grand Canyon itself, but also of its east rim, known as the Palisades of the Desert, a series of vertical scallops in the cliffs above us, tinted red by the sunset.

Over dinner we discussed yet another scheme for eclipse warning, which could have used those scallops in the cliffs. I'd worked it out back in rainy Seattle, while planning the expedition. In reading about Pueblo lore, I'd been struck with their notion of an underworld—and decided that the concept might substitute in some ways for what we call solid geometry. I even found a practical use for their underworld.

> [*One of the fundamental elements of Hopi world view is*] *the concept of a dual division of time and space between the upper world of the living and the lower world of the dead. This is expressed in the description of the sun's journey on its daily rounds. The Hopi believe that the sun has two entrances, variously referred to as houses, homes or kivas, situated at each extremity of its course. In the morning the sun is said to emerge from its eastern house, and in the evening it is said to descend into its western home. During the night the sun must travel underground from west to east in order to be ready to arise at its accustomed place the next day. Hence day and night are reversed in the upper and lower worlds. . . .*
>
> the anthropologist Mischa Titiev, 1944

THE YEAR HAS A DUALITY FOR THE PUEBLO PEOPLES, quite in addition to the day-night duality: an underworld is said to duplicate the real world, but it's a half-year in advance of the real world. Thus, "When the winter Powa-moon is shining in the Above (that is, in the world where we live), its counterpart the . . . summer Powa-moon is shining in the Below."

The Hopi calendar in use in the nineteenth century had a peculiarity that fits well with yet another lunar-eclipse-warning scheme. In the old Hopi calendar, the winter months were called by the same names as the summer months. You may remember in the Pekwin story that the Zuni's sun god said, "At the end of the year when I come to the south, watch me closely; and in the middle of the year in the *same* month . . . , watch me closely" (my emphasis). To illustrate, the first month after each solstice was called *Pa-muya* at Hopi. It is as if we were to call both January and July by the same name (say, "Januly"), both February and August by another name ("Febgust"), etc.

That is a very odd arrangement, since Hopi ceremonies throughout the year are scheduled by when the sun rises or sets over some horizon feature (with some modification by what the moon is doing that year). Yet these month names do not directly correspond to horizon positions—*Pa-muya* occurs when the sunrise is in both the most extreme south-east and the extreme northeast sectors of the swing in sunrise between *120°* and *60°*, but only in the month after the sol-stice, not before it (when the sunrise is also in the same sector). Such peculiar month names suggest a second calen-dar system superimposed upon the sensible horizon calendar system. Why?

Horizon calendars are rather like measuring the eastern horizon with a ruler, marked off with the days since the last solstice. When the sun rises over this ruler, you read off the date. It's not a linear scale (the 31 days of March will occupy far more space than the 31 days of January, for example), but linearity is important only if you need to add and subtract. If you just want to *compare* two arcs that each start from a solstice, so as to pronounce them same-or-different, the non-linearity won't bother you.

Now, suppose that you treat the full moon as if it were the rising sun, and read off its "date" from the horizon scale: you merely *measure the full moon with the sun's ruler.* "The moon's in the middle of March," as we could say if the moonrise was nearly due east, where the sun rises in mid-March. Given the similarity in size and shape between the sun and the full moon, one can see how this practice might have gotten started without an intent to predict eclipses—especially given that underworld notion. If the moon's date (the number of "days" from the other solstice extreme) is the same as the sun's current date, eclipses will tend to occur: the moon's "date" is simply the angle from the *other* solstice, just as the sun's date is the angle from the most recent solstice.

Suppose that it was a month after the winter solstice, and that the moon rose where the sun does a month after the summer solstice: the "date" of each is the "last day of January." Since the "January" month is just a stand-in for an angle, you've got the condition for an eclipse.

Thus a simple eclipse warning scheme, requiring no understanding of Hoyle's equal angles principle, is to *measure the full moon with the sun's ruler and watch out for "identical" dates.*

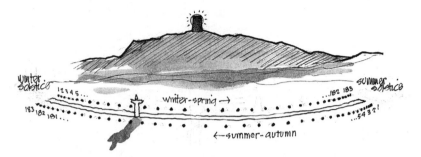

It's nothing more than Method #7 ("The Arm's-Length Necklace") but using the most recent solstice rather than the nearest solstice, using the horizon's features rather than a necklace. Ambiguity has its uses, in Method #12: "Measuring the Moon with the Sun's Horizon Calendar."

Comparing dates circumvents the usual problem of correcting the sunrise angle for the local horizon elevation—or of leveling the horizon, which would defeat the naming of those notches that prove so handy for a horizon calendar. You're not literally measuring the angle between sunrise and solstice sightline, in the manner of holding a necklace up, but using the date as a stand-in for the true angle. Indeed, the bumpier the horizon the better, as the ruler will require less interpolation between named features.

LACKING THE PALISADES OF THE DESERT OR A SIMI-larly bumpy skyline, you can use the pivot method from Perfect Kiva, discussed again at Tsin Kletzin: the observer pivots around a tower to keep the rising sun almost hidden. The wider the tower, the larger the observer's circle would have to be (you have to get far enough back so the tower appears only a half-degree wide, the same as the sun). And long lever arms make the daily sidesteps especially obvious. Each day of the half-year would have its own viewing position.

You could, I suppose, create a series of 183 marks, one for each day, and number them somehow, starting at the winter solstice ("Number 1") so that "Winter-Spring #183" was at the summer solstice sunrise rising position. For convenience, put them all on one side of the well-trodden path, say the side facing the pivot. Then create another series of 183 stones for summer-autumn on the back side of the path, numbered with the days after the summer solstice until reaching the winter solstice stone ("Summer-Autumn #183"). Your observer path is bordered by numbered stones. *If the sun rises when the priest is standing at Winter-Spring stone 67, then the eclipse-prone position for moonrise will be near Summer-Autumn stone 67.* Well, you could be off by a day because of the earth's elliptical orbit, but I suppose that this counts as Method #13, "Moon Date Equals Sun Date" (though I'd bet that a name involving a coincidence with underworld happenings would be more likely, were the Anasazi using the method).

Furthermore, you need not count the 183 days of the half-year in an unbroken string. Any scheme of subdividing the half-year will do (such as the Januly-type names), so long as it begins and ends with a solstice. It need not be keyed exactly to a solstice. A fixed time after a solstice will also suffice, as when the month ends ten days after a solstice in our present calendar system (note that our modern January and July both start approximately when the standstill is over). The descriptions of the old Hopi calendar certainly come close to these requirements, though the overlay of new moon considerations complicates the issue (like the Romans, the Hopi tried to incorporate new moons somehow into a solar-synchronized calendar).

This potential use of the old month-naming scheme makes me wonder if the Hopi or their ancestors managed to find a method that merged an eastern-horizon-only eclipse-warning scheme (that ordinarily requires a flattened horizon) with the otherwise desirable bumpy-horizon seasonal calendar for agriculture. Compromises for calendar reform, which somehow merge the features of two calendar systems, have taken many generations to work out in European cultures. No one knows how long the Maya spent trying to mesh their 260-day ceremonial calendar (arguably related to magic number schemes) with the 365.24-day seasonal calendar—but one speculates that it stimulated their need for more and better mathematical methods. If the Anasazi merged a bumpy-horizon seasonal calendar with a flat-horizon eclipse-forecasting system, the feat surely ranks high among prehistoric intellectual accomplishments.

If the Pueblo peoples warn of eclipses using this horizon calendar scheme (or any other), they have successfully kept it a secret from the anthropologists. Whenever I think of Pueblo secrecy in ritual matters, I am reminded of the Pythagoreans, whose penalties were severe for disclosing even the existence of the dodecahedron. There is, of course, the possibility that the natives did tell the anthropologists—but that the anthropologists knew less astronomy than the natives, and so were never able to make sense of the explanations offered (such has occurred in matters biological, where natives accurately distinguish between sibling species of plants that most knowledgeable observers lump together). Indeed, even if a knowledgeable Pueblo shaman had undertaken to explain all to an astronomer, the explanation might have gone unappreciated, as approximate methods are unknown to most astronomers.

> The Hopi orientation bears no relation to North and South, but to the points on the horizon which mark the places of sunrise and sunset at the summer and winter solstices. He invariably begins his ceremonial circuit by pointing (1) to the place of sunset at summer solstice, next to (2) the place of sunset at winter solstice, then to (3) the place of sunrise at winter solstice, and (4) the place of sunrise at summer solstice, &c. . . . Doesn't that please you? . . . As soon as it flashed upon me, I hastened in to apply the key to some of the old fellows' knowledge boxes. And then they one and all declared how glad they were that I now understood, how sorry they had been *that I could not understand this simple fact before.*
>
> the ethnographer ALEXANDER M. STEPHEN, 1893

WHEN DAWN COMES TO THE GRAND CANYON, A CUR-
tain of light slowly falls into the rugged valley. From our
campsite halfway down the South Rim, the warm morning
light first shines on the topmost cliffs of the North Rim—
indeed, exactly where I stood at Cape Royal trying to follow
my shadow at sunset.

The curtain of light drifts downward in a stately manner, revealing more and more of the nighttime canyon still in
shadow. Dawn in the Canyon is a world of red cliffs, of
whitened spires, of chocolate-colored buttes shaped like temples and castles. Sunrise can take more than an hour to sweep
down from rim to river. It is a special hour when the air is
still and clear, where the rich colors and long shadows contrast, emphasizing the depth and detail of the Canyon.

Sunrise follows Unkar Creek down from its beginnings
below Cape Royal, slowly bringing a new day to one after
another of the dwelling places of the Anasazi; their corn
patches were scattered all along the length of that creek,
wherever a seep provided enough water. Eventually the sun
reaches the sandy slopes near the river at Unkar Delta.

Then the sun illuminates Cardenas hilltop across the
river. Inside the mile-deep Canyon, this is a minor hill,
distinguished only by its enigmatic ruin. The hilltop's view
is sweeping and spectacular, a panorama of the Canyon and
its rims. But its exposed position, atop a windswept ridge
well away from water supplies, is hardly the sensible building
site usually favored by the Anasazi. It's too large for a mere
scout's lookout and, although the Pueblo peoples do build
prayer shrines in distant places, well away from their habitations, I've never heard of one quite so large. A kiva for Unkar
Delta peoples?

> At the edge of the mesas some ten kilometers across the
> valley to the southeast from each Hopi village there
> stood . . . a small shrine called *Tawaki*, or Sun's
> house. . . . [The] shrines are small, easily disturbed, and
> bear few of the criteria to give them much credence as

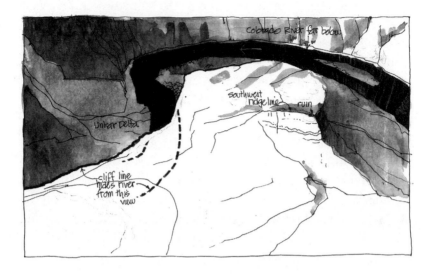

distant foresights, except that we are told that they are, and the direction in which they lie confirms this. The one element that does stand out is the sacredness of such sites. . . . Each year when the Sun arrives at his [Winter house], prayer sticks [**Pathos**] adorned with feathers and other ritual symbols are made to be offered to the Sun. . . . During the period of four days when the Sun is said to stay at his house, these offerings are deposited at the shrine by one of the younger members of the society responsible for the solstice ceremonies.

the historian STEPHEN C. MCCLUSKEY, 1982

Even without having visited Cardenas hilltop at sunrise, I can tell you (thanks to topographic maps and computers) that something very special happens near that place. Each day in midwinter, about the time that the descending curtain of sunlight reaches the river's edge, a narrow beam of light begins to shine on the hilltop. Like a dim and diffuse spotlight beaming down on a stage, a circle of sunlight illuminates the hilltop near the ruin. Each day as the winter solstice approaches, this spot of light brings a new day to the hilltop for a few special minutes before the wave of sunshine marching across the canyon reaches the hilltop. The next day, the spot of light comes a step or two closer to the ruin.

Looking up at the rocks that block the about-to-rise sun, observers would have seen a humanlike facial profile in the skyline, looking rather like an Indian chief gazing up into the sky. His "eye" would appear to be brightly lit (that's what causes the spotlight), and a "halo" appears around his "head." This probably did not escape the notice of the Anasazi, judging by the fascination that the winter solstice sunrise has for their descendants in the Pueblos, forty generations later. Did the beam of sunlight illuminate a waiting group of Anasazi, and signal the start of a solstice celebration?

THE PUEBLO PEOPLE DON'T CALL IT THE "WINTER solstice," of course. Their phrase translates as "the Sun's Winter House"—though the word "kiva" is sometimes used instead of "house." That's an unusual spatial metaphor for something that most of us treat as an event in time. It brings to mind some sort of structure, almost like a Swiss-German cuckoo clock to house the sun at its standstill. A Sun Priest dealing with a horizon calendar would be referencing some peak or notch in a skyline—and at Hopi, not even that. A climber's hut atop a mountain pass does not seem a likely structure to associate with the solstice sunrise. Even if the term "house" is mostly metaphor, surely there are antecedents in some other practice. And I think that I've found a candidate.

With levered sightlines pivoting about a foresight, where the observer moves every day to maintain a standard view of the rising sun, you can imagine a corral that marks the end of the line, the place where the Sun Priest stands still for days. A modern analogy would be the end-of-the-line turntable used to reverse a trolley car on its tracks—the trolley barn as kiva? Might the Cardenas Hilltop Ruin be such a turnaround? It all depends on whether the "eye" is indeed the pivot, part of an obscuring frame that forces the rising sun into a well-defined corner.

Could this have been a special kiva for the winter solstice—the Sun's Winter House? A real structure after all?

171

SUCH A PROSPECT IS HOW I GOT SIX FRIENDS TO carry heavy packs down icy slopes, to devote a week to helping satisfy my curiosity about this site in the bottom of the Grand Canyon.

Alan Fisk-Williams is the boatman (and lately high school science teacher) who introduced me to the place—and also introduced me to Bob Euler, who proved so helpful with anthropological background of the Grand Canyon's Anasazi. Alan organized the logistics, all that food for hungry people.

John DuBois is my oldest continuous friend, dating back to grade school near Kansas City, continuing through high school, through undergraduate years at Northwestern University; we even both did Ph.D. degrees in somewhat similar subjects, John in bioengineering and I in neurophysiology. John (who more recently has been designing instruments for orbiting satellites) was my source for all the computer programs that ran the heavens backward to tell me what things looked like in the past, ran them forward to tell me when to be where, if I wanted a good view. John's teenaged son Jim also came along from Boston; I'm not sure I'd want to do this as my first major hike, as it might make subsequent hikes pale by comparison.

Jack Bunn is another old friend from graduate school; we suffered through qualifying exams together. A Seattle eye surgeon, Jack has an ophthalmologist's eye for visual spectacle (as will become apparent). Two of his friends, Lynn Langley and Karen Kepler, were readily persuaded to come along as additional observers.

As we hiked down, we all kept a lookout for that hole-in-the-wall in Cardenas Butte. It couldn't be resolved on the topographic map, and the aerial photographs weren't much help either. What we saw were some blocky chunks of Supai formation in the shape of a letter "G"; no matter how hard we looked, we couldn't find an enclosed "O" in that rock formation.

Lunch was taken in the Precambrian layers, sitting on rocks that were 800 million years old. Then on to the Colo-

rado River, with a stop to refill the canteens. A few more miles downriver was our intended campsite, the same one that Alan and I had stayed in, back that night of the long lunar eclipse.

THE CARDENAS CAMPSITE IS ALONG THE COLORADO River at Mile 71, and we made camp there on the second afternoon, Jim and I arriving well ahead of the others.

I was curious whether a sunset sightline might exist at winter solstice, so Jim and I hurried to get up to the ruin before the sunset—which is rather early in the depths of the Grand Canyon in midwinter. Alan had told me about a shortcut trail that led directly up a ridgeline, beginning in back of the camp, and I quickly found it and puffed my way uphill. When I crested the top, I saw the Cardenas Hilltop Ruin in the late afternoon sunlight, looking even larger than it had in the pictures, certainly more sizable than I had remembered seeing it in the fading moonlight before that extra long lunar eclipse.

And there was the Cardenas Butte hole-in-the-wall, standing above the ruin in the southeast, blue sky clearly visible through it, even without the aid of binoculars. The

173

Cardenas Butte as seen from the hilltop near Cardenas ruin. The window is located just to the right of the V-notch at the center of the photograph.

rocks surrounding it were perfectly lit by the setting sun, as clear a view as we ever had. The hole-in-the-wall, I realized, was indeed the "G" we had seen from the trail on our descent. From down here, the view of it was so oblique that the "G" appeared closed like an "O." The hole-in-the-wall that isn't. But in this case, the appearance is what counts—a virtual hole, perhaps? Maybe just "window" will do.

The sunset itself was considerably less interesting. It merely set into the side of a butte, at no special place. We checked in with the others by radio; they had arrived at camp too late to start uphill. And I talked with Katherine up on the rim, who said the weather ought to be good tomorrow morning—but maybe not the day after, the exact day of the winter solstice. Another storm system was coming.

Dinner was hurried. Briefing for the morning's activities was done by flashlight, over the sound of the rushing river.

IN THE MIDDLE OF THE NIGHT, ALAN AND I WERE awakened by some animal repeatedly jumping up the side of the tent and sliding back down. Alan looked out the little crescent of tent flap that we'd left unzipped for ventilation, up near the top of the dome tent. Outside, staring back into the flashlight, was a rather large rat, poised to jump in through that opening. Alan spoke to the rat firmly.

The next day, I discovered that my shiny metal spoon was missing. That was one determined packrat; I'm surprised that it didn't try to acquire Alan's flashlight for its collection. The archaeologists are rather fond of packrats, at least in the abstract: they hoard seeds and nuts (and anything shiny, for unknown reasons), but don't always consume them. So the archaeologists can mine their middens, dating them with radiocarbon techniques, using the plants that were growing in the various millennia as an indicator of ancient climate change.

Maybe some future archaeologist will find my spoon, stashed away in some recess in the rocks. We carried lots of extra batteries—for the cameras, for John's little computer, for the flashlights, for the two handheld radios, for the little tape recorders—but not an extra spoon. Eating breakfast cereal with a fork is not my idea of fun.

> All wood rats are good house-builders, but white-throated wood rats are among the best. They cut branches, cactus pads, and leaves to incorporate in their houses. Then they pick up anything loose to add to the structure—bottles, cans, mule droppings, bones, papers, or even mouse-traps. Houses may be as much as 4 feet high with numerous entrances opening to a maze of tunnels which end up at the inner nest. . . . All wood rats are excellent climbers and debark the limbs of bushes of all sizes.
>
> from DONALD F. HOFFMEISTER,
> *Mammals of the Grand Canyon*, 1971

WE HAD A LOT OF QUESTIONS TO ANSWER IN ONLY two mornings—and the second morning might be too cloudy to utilize. So there was a certain amount of "spreading our bets" that first morning, a day before the solstice.

What it meant was spreading our seven observers all of the way along the hilltop ridgeline that ran from the ruin in a southwesterly direction.

As best as I could tell from the calculations, the ruin wasn't the best place to see the sunrise spectacle anymore: that was surely somewhere to the southwest of it. Even if the ruin were the best place a thousand years ago, the 0.1° reduction in the tilt of the earth's axis since then would have shifted the final viewpoint about 10 meters to the southwest.

What we might see could be predicted to some extent: The Cardenas Butte skyline, elevated 15° from the ridgeline, has a U-shaped "notch" to the north of the hole-in-the-wall (the "window"). The sun would peek through this notch, while otherwise remaining obscured behind the rocks, and this might last for a half-minute if the observer didn't move. Then the window would brighten. After some seconds of the brilliant silhouette of the facial profile with the gleaming window, the sun crests the butte to the right of the window ("crest") and the scene becomes too bright to view. If one were to stand too close to the ruin, the sun would merely rise over the notch, and the scene would be too bright for further viewing; you'd have to move to your right to keep from being blinded. If you moved too far right, you'd never see the window lighted before the sun crested the butte. So in between, you should be able to keep the sun obscured except for that window.

John and I both had small tape recorders on wrist straps and good telephoto lenses; we planned to move around to try and find the best view. Rather than fiddling with maps or aerial photos, we decided to mark the spots at which we shot pictures or dictated observations by dropping numbered coins on the ground; that would allow us to reconstruct the sunrise scene afterward. The other five stationary observers were scattered over 140 meters of the ridgeline.

I stayed near the ruin myself, looking at the brightening ridgeline with the big telephoto lens on my camera. But I guessed wrong. Jack Bunn shouted "Notch!" and then side-

Aerial photograph of Cardenas hilltop. The rectangular ruin is visible at the tricuspid intersection to the right of center. The ridgeline at ten o'clock runs northeast to southwest and is the observer path in the month before and after winter solstice.

stepped to the southwest for a better view, while John and I ran toward him. Soon the sun crested the butte, and it was all over. Most of us had missed the view. Everyone commented on the strong "halo" around all of the skyline features near the sun—and maybe something spiky in addition.

Jack had dropped a Canadian five-cent coin on the ground before he moved; it turned out to be 79 meters from the ruin. He thought that the best place to view the lighted window was several meters southwest along the ridgeline. And Jack had picked the 79-meter spot by a different criterion from mine. I'd been busy, watching the brightening skyline. He turned around and watched the shadow line moving toward our ridgeline, spotted the distorted features of the skyline we were watching, and maneuvered himself near to where he thought the window view would be. I never thought to look behind me; scientists often become fixated on a plan, but lots of the interesting discoveries come from just keeping alert, looking around for incidental things, like creeping shadows.

So, we now knew where to stand tomorrow, a line of observers closely spaced, far from the ruin. After debriefing was complete, we hiked over to see the Colorado River from atop the cliffs. Unkar Delta across the river was newly bathed in morning sunlight, and Alan pointed out the ruins and where the Anasazi had irrigated fields of corn and squash. But I was restless to get back to camp, wanting to use John's computer to figure out the significance of that 79-meter distance. It was far longer than I had guessed, and it was a good thing that I'd spread the observers widely rather than clustered them near my preliminary estimated position, about 10 meters from the ruin.

Essentially, the question was: How much more must the earth's axis be tilted to move Jack's observer position inside the ruin? Was it too much, more than the known estimates of the earth's range of tilt fluctuations (24.6° is about the greatest)? That would certainly scuttle the Sun's Winter House hypothesis for the Cardenas Hilltop Ruin. John and I sat on a log next to the river and tapped the numbers into the hand-held computer in order to get a rough estimate. It said that the tilt would have to be nearly a degree beyond the present 23.43°. So, while uncomfortably large (i.e., a long, long time ago), not entirely impossible.

We had a radio schedule to talk with Bob Euler up on the South Rim, and I reported our preliminary findings. And got the revised weather forecast: probably clear tomorrow for the solstice, but with snow arriving soon after. That suggested that we weren't going to get a third morning at the ruin, that we would need to hike out starting tomorrow, after the sunrise.

STANDSTILL SUGGESTS THAT THE BEST VIEWER POSI-tion ought not to change from the day before the solstice to the actual morning of the solstice, but the 3,100-meter (two

mile) long Cardenas sightline produces an extraordinary am-
plification of even slight changes in horizon position of the
sun, causing the standard view to shift 0.5 meters toward the
ruin, about a sidestep worth for the observer. During the two
weeks before the solstice, the viewing position changes 67
meters (nearly half a city block). About 17 meters of that
occurs in the last seven mornings; the daily sidesteps should
be 4.4, 3.8, 3.1, 2.3, 1.6, 0.9, and 0.5 meters. Then it re-
verses.

If an observer could detect the difference that half a
meter made, then the exact day of the winter solstice could be
determined, even before the reversal, just because you'd
reach the daily markers left from previous turnarounds. The
sensitivity of the viewing position was the other important
thing we'd need to find out, in our one remaining morning; it
tells you how big a circle you need for a pivot calendar (as in
Method #13) that can discern each and every day of the year
via a stone circle.

Part of the day was spent measuring distances from ruin
to ridgeline, calibrating the aerial photographs that Katherine and I had taken from a small airplane several days
earlier. And we looked around the ruin and along the
ridgeline for ancient markers of any sort: carved rocks would
have been nice, but I would have settled for tally marks.
Nothing. Of course, a rock cairn will suffice for a century
and, given the way that the turnaround (and all the other
daily markers) would have drifted away from the ruin at the
rate of about one meter per century, rock inscriptions would
have become inaccurate here in only a few generations of Sun
Priests. At sites such as Perfect Kiva, where the lever arm is
19-fold shorter (and thus the daily movements, and the century movements), viewer positions would have likely seemed
eternal.

Archaeologists have never excavated Cardenas hilltop,
so we have no idea what the rock underlying the ruin might
contain. Perhaps there are little buried offerings in some
recesses in the rock floor, analogous to the prayer sticks

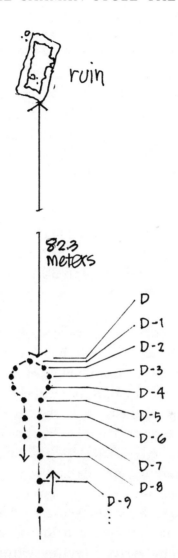

(containing many bird feathers) that the Pueblo peoples leave at isolated shrines? Then too, the packrats might have created a time capsule: I keep hoping that the pre-Pueblo prayer sticks contain materials attractive to packrats—perhaps crystal or mica? Maybe a piñon nut necklace, so that a packrat might save a radiocarbon-datable nut with flattened ends and a hole through it? I could learn to like packrats.

SOLSTICE DAY ARRIVED AFTER A BETTER NIGHT'S sleep than the previous night; our modern packrat, genus

Neotoma, seemed to have heeded Alan's admonition. Perhaps the packrat was too busy admiring his recent acquisitions.

Now that we knew approximately where to stand along the ridgeline, we could cluster. I tried for several meters apart, hoping to answer the sensitivity questions. John and I synchronized our watches with my camera back that imprinted the time on each color picture that I took. We tested our pocket tape recorders, making sure that everyone's voice could be heard.

This time I used Jack's trick, watching the sunrise shadow creeping slowly across the Colorado River, then up toward us. It's sure hard to see the "spotlight" itself, in the manner of Delicate Arch's; with 3-kilometer distances, the shadow edges become pretty fuzzy, as I should have guessed. But the horizon's "profile" can be identified from the shadow line and so you can guess where to stand.

About that time, I realized that this sunrise spectacle on the hilltop is also visible from down below, on the riverbank. The right place would be just a mile or so upriver from Unkar Delta, and on the route to the other agricultural sites on that side of the river. Back before the Glen Canyon Dam started regulating river flows, the river thinned down considerably in midwinter, and the exposed river channel would have dried out and made an excellent footpath through this part of the Grand Canyon, an Anasazi "Main Street." Maybe that's how they discovered this halo-and-window spectacle, just walking along the river, anytime in the month before or the month after the winter solstice. Perhaps the priests reserved the hilltop for themselves after trying to build the Sun's Winter House where the spring floods washed it away.

Alan, standing farther toward the ruin than the rest of us, caught the first glimpse of the sun but soon all observers were reporting the sun in the notch. One minute later, John reported seeing the sun in all three places: notch, window, and crest. But just 2.1 meters southwest of John, I saw none of this—yet 15 seconds later, I saw (and photographed) a magnificent sight: *Only the window was brightly lit, with wispy curls silhouetting the rest of the "facial profile."* Solar corona? Karen and Lynn, standing 1.3 meters farther southwest than I was, saw only the bright wisps, without the window lit.

Then everyone was reporting "crest" and we stopped looking. I handed the camera with the telephoto to Alan, who was wearing his running shoes rather than his climbing boots. We wanted a photograph of sunrise from the ruin, just to show how far off sunrise position was from the interesting spectacle. He took off for the ruin, making the trip in only 36 seconds—then had to wait for two minutes before the sun finally rose at the ruin. Sunrise there was considerably to the left of the low point in the horizon.

Anticlimax. We began debriefing each observer, then measuring the positions of the numbered coins that marked their various positions along the ridgeline. As the roving observer, I had dropped six coins, announcing each into the tape recorder.

A moving observer would have about 90 seconds to position the sun behind the rocks: one is forced southwest because the left edge of the sun peeks out and becomes too bright to view. If one goes too far southwest, the window isn't lit. If I were an Anasazi observer trying to define a standard view to use each morning, I'd first find a place where only the notch is illuminated, then move right just far enough to keep it dimly lit. The notch would darken as the window brightened. Finally, the window would wink out before the sun finally crested the butte.

My guess is that an experienced observer (and they got lots of practice, in the month before and after the solstice) could become pretty good at finding the viewpoint for this sequence. He could sidestep left, and recognize the view as a bit wrong; sidestep a bit right, only to correct back. It's an empirical question, but I'll bet that less than a 0.5-meter uncertainty in "the right place" would remain after a little practice, thanks to how well the notch–window–crest combination serves to precisely corner the half-degree-diameter sun in an obscuring frame.

That suggests a standstill of several days, when the observer can't be sure if reversal has occurred—but if the observer had a series of rock cairns marking a week of viewing positions from a prior year of unclouded sunrises, then just one unclouded sunrise would suffice to predict the exact day of turnaround. When the daily sidesteps are several meters, and the positioning uncertainty is less than a meter, it's pretty easy to know which presolstice day you're at.

And this also suggests that 3,100 meters is sufficient as the lever arm, if you want to create one of those pivot calendars with an observer path that is lined with 183 stones on each side. Expert observers might get by with much shorter distances to the pivot.

SUBSEQUENT ANALYSIS OF THE SUNRISE PHOTOGRAPHS showed that those wisps on the skyline couldn't be solar corona, as they didn't move when the sun rose further. It was just vegetation growing around the "G" window, strongly backlit. When windblown—or back in the days when Grand Canyon vegetation was denser—it must have been an even more impressive embellishment on the sunrise peeking through the window.

The turnaround is currently 82.3 meters along the path from the nearest corner of the ruin, using my proposed standard view. To run things back in time, I had to allow for the ruin being 7.4 meters lower in elevation than the ridgeline viewpoint (which I estimated from photographs), and for the Anasazi being 0.3 meters shorter (on average) than I am. But the result was that the present site of the ruin could indeed have been a turnaround during the period since Paleo-Indians began visiting the high desert Southwest. It could be a Sun's Winter House, a place where the Sun Priest stood still.

But it would have to be a very old one. The date suggested is back within a millennium of when the tilt of the earth's axis was near its most recent maximum, 9,500 years ago. Since then, the winter solstice viewpoint has been slowly drifting away from the site of the ruin; the tilt cycle is

41,000 years long and so it will continue to flee the ruin for some time yet.

The ruin surrounds the turnaround of all turnarounds (whether or not the Paleo-Indians knew it), the Ultimate Turnaround. The Kiva of all kivas? The holiest of the Holy?

I certainly doubt that the present ruin is 9,500 years old. Bob Euler has compared photographs taken a century ago with the present state of the ruin, and thinks that there is little change from a century's wear and tear. Still, I'd expect it had to be rebuilt every millennium or so, just from the windstorms; the walls are only piled-up slabs of stone (from a nearby outcrop) that a few workers could build in a few days. No mortar, no roof—more like a New England rock fence. The issue is whether this might be a traditional site, preserved and occasionally maintained, even though the solstice turnaround kept drifting farther away.

It's not as improbable as it initially seems. Paleo-Indians were around the higher elevations of the Southwest by that date, the Clovis-Folsom hunters that were likely Arctic-adapted prior to the opening of the ice-free corridor through Canada about 12,000 years ago. About 10,000 years ago, the transition from big-game hunting to foraging occurred, as the megafauna disappeared. The mild temperatures, plus the good hunting and gathering, would have surely attracted them into this part of the bottom of the Grand Canyon during the winter storms. And the lighted window in Cardenas Butte is a visual spectacle that is easily discovered for several months of midwinter, just walking along the river's "Main Street" about sunrise. So it's not unlikely that the Paleo-Indians viewed winter solstice sunrise hereabouts, not unlikely that they saw the spectacle.

Thus, for the ruin to be a Sun's Winter House, it would have to be a particularly old one. The archaeoastronomy suggests that the rock crevasses around Cardenas hilltop might be a good place to search by more traditional archaeological methods. I just hope that the ancient Paleo-Indians (or the ancient packrats) left us some time capsules.

10

The Long Ascent: From Shaman to Scientist

It is when we take some interest in the great discoverers and their lives that [science] becomes endurable, and only when we begin to trace the development of ideas that it becomes fascinating.

the nineteenth-century physicist
JAMES CLERK MAXWELL

Hiking upriver two hours after sunrise, I looked back from my first rest stop—and had difficulty even locating the Cardenas hilltop amidst the other shapes of the Grand Canyon.

It had become cloudy but remained shirtsleeve hiking weather. The mild winter temperatures in the bottom of the Grand Canyon can be compared to a marine climate like that of Seattle or San Francisco, where the sea temperature usually keeps adjacent land from cooling down to freezing even in winter. As temperate zone winters go, conditions are pleasant. The animals know it too, judging from the footprints that you occasionally see, leading down to the shores of the Colorado River. Still, you can look up at the North Rim and see tall snowdrifts.

EXCITING AS WAS OUR VISIT TO CARDENAS, A RENAISsance in naked-eye astronomy isn't what motivates my search. Nor am I trying to demonstrate unequivocally that prehistoric peoples indeed utilized one of these methods. Rather, I want to establish that there are so many routes to the serendipitous discovery of eclipse forecasting that it is unreasonable to assume that protoscientific practices awaited the coming of civilization.

The fact that there are so many eclipse methods suggests that there are multiple routes to this kind of knowledge base, that it need not require the specialized roles and record-keeping that we imagine existing only after the settled existence associated with agriculture. Indeed, one can even argue that hunter-gatherer eclipse-warning success might have promoted a settlement near useful horizon features, the shaman reluctant to move very far away from where the methods seemed to work—and that agriculture was promoted by such settlement.

Was supernaturalism part of all this? Supernaturalism is merely the social give-and-take metaphor, carried to extremes. For nearly all humans, that's the "mechanism" that they know best: they learn it from their siblings, they often consciously use it as young adults in trying to make their way in a world where older adults control the resources. When you have to deal with something that you don't understand, you don't invent something out of the clear blue sky. The first thing that you try is a familiar analogy—and for most people, that's social give-and-take. These days, many of us have additional mechanistic metaphors: we apply plumbing ("He's stuck"), photographic ("A virtual snapshot in time"), automotive ("She's a real self-starter"), and sailboat analogies ("He keeps flip-flopping on the issue") that not only broaden our social analyses but also allow us insights into harder-to-understand physical systems such as electricity, aerodynamics, computers, and ocean currents. In science, we have gradually developed an extensive repertoire of analogies, handy for trying out on new situations to see if they will give some insight, even if they won't work exactly: even mentally, you can't make something out of nothing, so you start with new combinations of old concepts.

Praying before an eclipse was just another supernatural application—but, with a forecast to trigger the suppliants, there would have been rapid feedback (that partial eclipse reversing instead of becoming total) before you forgot the antecedents. The role of the priests with the skills to warn of eclipses would come to be recognized, in a way with few parallels in the usual supernaturalistic pleading for rainfall, for prey animals to come one's way, and so forth. That's a lot of incentive for the priests to improve their predictive skills.

The only other shamanistic activity with a good parallel to eclipse forecasting is the physician's good fortune, being able to take credit for the patient spontaneously getting better. As all physicians eventually learn, most illnesses—at least, at the stage when the patient initially seeks out a physician—really are better the next morning, even without treatment (that's why you always have to compare a new therapy to the "natural course" of the disease if left untreated—and disease symptoms often fluctuate). So too, after most ritual forms of healing, the shaman probably got a lot of undeserved credit from patients who spontaneously improved.

BEFORE THE TRAIL TURNED UPHILL, WE DIPPED OUR water bottles into the Colorado River, loaded up with a two-day supply. It was a dry trail ahead—except, of course, for the ice. And that predicted snow. The sun was no longer shining and the skies had become gray.

The age of the Cardenas ruin continued to intrigue me, as I hiked uphill. One millennium versus ten is certainly an enigmatic aspect of the Cardenas levered sightline. But the significance of the Cardenas lever—as well as that at Perfect Kiva and anywhere else with a good corner in which to fit the sun—doesn't really depend on age. It's all those implications for how early instrumented science could have evolved, could have provided some metaphors that would serve as new building blocks: counting, comparison, measurement. One tends to credit curiosity about how nature works, but most societies were probably not like the ancient Greeks in

that regard. Environmental situations that shape discovery—
so that you can "back into" a method without really intending to—may represent an earlier stage of protoscience than
intellectual curiosity about the nonedible aspects of nature.

IF AN OBSERVATORY IS "A PLACE EQUIPPED FOR THE
measurement of natural phenomena," it seems particularly
appropriate to call Cardenas a natural observatory rather
than merely a sun-watching station. The measuring instrument emerges from properties of the terrain (the window is
the pivot, the ridgeline is analogous to the calibrated arc of a
sextant)—the sextant as *objet trouvé*?

Shadows are "light levers," the shadow edge rotating
about a fulcrum as the sun rises. With long lever arms, one
might expect considerable sensitivity to small-angle changes
in solar declination near the solstice. Yet shadows per se have
their problems, even in a large room such as a great kiva. The
penumbra of the half-degree-wide sun is nearly one percent
of the lever arm, blurring the shadow boundary as distance
increases. That's why I think that all those shadow tricks
using caves and rock art are analogous to toy sundials. Maybe
they were used, and were part of the learning curve before
more precision methods were invented, but most shadow
spectacles are likely imitations of a sort.

A major improvement is to watch the sun rather than
the shadow, framing it somehow to get the advantages of
leverage. The open frame, such as winter solstice sunrise at
the Hungo Pavi kiva, does have a problem (though it is
minor, compared to watching shadows). Because framing
the side and bottom of the exposed sun is possible only at
elevations near the horizontal, the results are going to vary
with the weather. Cold, dense air serves to bend light better;
when the sun appears to be sitting on the local horizon
(which itself is not particularly bent), it is actually farther
below the horizontal than usual—and therefore farther
north. Conversely a heat wave can move the sunrise southeasterly, even make you think that the solstice has arrived

prematurely. It must have been embarrassing for a Sun Priest when, in retrospect, the solstice was celebrated on the wrong day.

Obscuring frames mean that the measurement can be made with the sun 15° high in the sky as at Perfect Kiva and Cardenas, where daily fluctuations in temperature, pressure, and humidity will produce little effect (because the light path through the atmosphere is much shorter). Combining obscuring-frames with pivoting-to-a-standard-view seems to be a particularly nice combination: it creates a uniform horizon (at least for the months that the frame and observation arc is useful), it avoids the aforementioned refraction fluctuations, and it allows just one unclouded morning in the week before the solstice to pinpoint the exact day, provided you can count on your fingers.

With lever arms the length of the Cardenas sightline, you can even detect leap-year-type fluctuations. You establish markers for the tenth, ninth, eighth, etc., mornings before the solstice. You use different colored stones the next year, and discover the drift. Which continues until, on the fourth year, you find yourself back over the original markers.

WE STRUGGLED UP THROUGH THE REDWALL CLIFFS IN the late afternoon and found a campsite on the back side of Cardenas Butte. Jim went exploring while dinner was cooking. He came back to announce to his father that he had found a cave—and was going to sleep in it.

It started raining early the next morning. Jim stayed a lot drier than the rest of us. In the morning light, we could see the fresh snow falling at lighter elevations—up where we were heading.

Alan intentionally didn't stir the pot where the oatmeal was cooking, just long enough to demonstrate how the surface would become furrowed into six-sided cells. Having seen some lava that had formed hexagonal columns, he wanted to demonstrate how six-sided columns simply emerged as a solution to a packing problem when there was a temperature gradient. Crystals do the same thing.

There were some big, wet snowflakes drifting down into the coffee cups. And surely sticking up higher along the trail. I talked to Katherine on the radio: She had been surveying some little-known Anasazi ruins that overlook this part of the Canyon, set back slightly from the South Rim—a summer home for the Cardenas Anasazi rather like those on the North Rim could have served for the Unkar Delta people?

And, she said, it's supposed to snow until Christmas Day.

OBSERVATORIES, EVEN NATURAL ONES, NEED PEOPLE. Who were these super shamans, on their way to becoming prophets? While eclipse prediction was, at some point, a powerful new tool for the shaman, the other skills of the shaman probably have deeper roots. To trace the development of ideas, it might be helpful to consider the non-astronomical skills that were likely involved in becoming a shaman or forecasting an eclipse.

The shaman as healer surely has its origins in mothering. The identification and use of natural medicines seems to be present even in chimpanzees; again, I would tend to expect that women were the experts because they spend a lot more time foraging for plant foods in most present-day pre-agricultural societies.

A lot of spatial intelligence is required for most of the eclipse methods; such mental abilities tend to be better developed in modern males than females—though the many female airline pilots with the requisite skills for one of the most spatially demanding tasks of the modern world (and a lot of men who can't find their car in the airport parking lot) demonstrate that gender isn't a reliable guide to expertise. Women tend to excel in verbal intelligence and, to the extent that storytelling was important to the role, might have been somewhat more likely to become a shaman than males.

Another aspect is the use of eclipse knowledge to dominate others. In the apes, males tend to use spectacular feats to manipulate the whole troop. Among the wild chimps at Gombe, Mike's charging display using the noisy tumbling of the tin cans is the classic example of attracting "respect" with a novel act. While there is a separate dominance hierarchy among chimp females, status is largely acquired by being born to a high-ranking mother, not by marvels that manipulate (though such tentative conclusions are always being overturned; when the number of observation hours doubles again, perhaps we will have seen some contrary examples).

Who has the spare time to devote to experimenting with sun and moon observation? Men tend to have more leisure time (certainly in the pueblos), and are better able to go wandering around the countryside without having to worry about dependent children. Many native societies (and some major world religions, such as Islam) severely restrict the mobility of females with culturally imposed rules.

I'm not so much interested in whether the protoscientific shamans were mostly male or mostly female, but I am interested in how a mix of skills coalesced into a part-time occupational specialization called "shaman." Among the useful talents are spatial-reasoning skills, plan-ahead skills, dominance-seeking tactics, methods for intimidating enemies, healing techniques, finding and using medicinal plants, weather forecasting, orchestrating spectacular performances, fortune-telling, spellbinding storytelling—and, of course, skills special to evoking the religious experience in listeners. But not every shaman would possess all such skills. Was there once a healing shaman (often female) and a separate spectacle-orchestrating shaman (often male) as the cultural niche started to evolve?

And when did a shaman become known as a prophet or seer (with their foresight connotations)? Surely the occasional success of eclipse forecasting must have lent authority to whatever the prophet had to say about other subjects. But it's a two-edged sword: Some people erroneously infer cause-

and-effect, equivalent to blaming a geologist for an earth-quake simply because the scientist predicted it. It's a version of the "bearer of bad news" effect: After something unusual happens, people tend to associate it unfavorably with the unusual things that happened even earlier. *Post hoc, ergo propter hoc* seems to apply even to predictions that precede the predicted event, in people without a more advanced understanding of cause and effect. If you predict good things, and they happen, you become associated with something good; a successful prediction of something bad is a little risky, and one suspects that prophet-protoscientists insulated themselves by claiming to be messengers rather than power brokers like Columbus.

THINKING ABOUT SHAMANISTIC PROTOSCIENCE DOES remind one of the modern versions of astrology, crystal power, numerology, fortune-telling, faith healing, and a variety of other rather tiresome fringe enterprises. They fascinate many people, and perhaps we will discover some clues to protoscience among them. Interfering with a modern scientist's interest in tracing the development of such ideas, however, are the pseudoscientific pretensions of the modern purveyors. While an educated subpopulation is relatively immune to their claims of power, they have media assistance in propagandizing the less experienced (and besides all their paid advertising, try comparing the column-inches that your local newspaper devotes weekly to astrology and to basic science).

The purveyors as a group are now somewhat different from when those subjects were part of the more general intellectual mainstream, back before things split apart into philosophy, religion, science, and fringe. The intellectual giants used to participate in the now-fringe discussions (Isaac Newton is a classic example from three centuries ago), back before they were recognized as dead ends. Improvements in eclipse prediction by Newton, for example, might have taken some of the fascination out of crystals (to the extent that they were useful for warning of total eclipses) and out of numerology (to the extent that some numerology was validated by those lists of magic numbers used by the Maya and the authors of Columbus's nautical almanac).

What we see now are remnants of the former spectrum of subject matter. Religion too is a remnant; if you can manage to ignore their creeds and concentrate instead on their deeds, you may notice that religions (television evangelists excepted) manage to provide civilizing services to the community that the snake-oil purveyors do not.

Why do people pay attention to the pseudoscientific fringe? Perhaps they perceive the power of knowledge but missed out in school on a decent science education—pseudoscience may be the best substitute that they can easily find, without going back to school (rather the way that comic books provide a refuge for the adult illiterate). I consider the popularity of pseudoscience (and those 94 percent levels of "scientific illiteracy") a reproach to the scientists, for our failure to convey the excitement of our subject in understandable terms, and a rebuke to the shortsighted legislators who starve our educational systems.

Science is often perceived as "difficult stuff," considerably worse than balancing your checkbook. That's a classic error: many mathematicians can't balance their checkbooks either. Besides, what most people want is an understanding of the world around them, not an ability to solve homework problems or dissect dead frogs, and so can be tempted by the shortcuts that pseudoscience claims to possess.

We also see how susceptible modern humans are to pseudoscientific claims: there is a niche for many of the aforementioned beliefs, one that continues to be exploited (sometimes cynically) by those who offer illusory shortcuts to knowledge and power. An orientation toward the future does bring with it a susceptibility to the false hopes raised by fortune-tellers. Our future-perfect thinking increases worry and suffering and gambling—but it is also a basis for our ethics.

197

To predict something without understanding why the prediction works may seem more like magic than science. But, it must be recalled, the same can still be said of most medical treatments for most diseases—aspirin was used for a hundred years before we even began to get some hints about how it functioned in the nervous system. While an eclipse prediction scheme such as "Clenched Fist" is crude by modern scientific standards, one presumes that combinations of several of these methods could have substantially improved the accuracy of prediction.

ASSUMING THAT THEY USED ONE OR MORE OF THE dozen methods, can we safely infer that it changed their society? Augmented the shaman's influence? Helped tribal levels of social organization evolve, maybe via the attractions of a spectacle-orchestrating shaman like Columbus? Helped the protoscientific and knowledgeable to occasionally triumph over the biggest and boldest, in struggles over leadership of a tribe?

Were we to see that an ancient culture had invented a form of gunpowder, we might reasonably conclude that it augmented the forms of social organization associated with warfare—though, lacking specific evidence, a stubborn skeptic could always argue that explosive power led to nothing more than firecrackers. Should the archaeologists see the features of these modestly accurate eclipse forecasting practices in an ancient culture, it will be interesting to debate what uses were made of predictive power. Perhaps such techniques only served to line the pockets of fortune-tellers rather than serving to manipulate masses of people, facilitate the beginnings of large-scale social organization, and reinforce religious practices. But I think it reasonable to assume that eclipse forecasting could have triggered some such changes.

Not only could predictive physical science have developed before the mathematics and geometry of the ancient

Greeks and Chinese, but it could have flourished long before organized record-keeping, potentially back in hunter-gatherer times, during the long haul of the ice ages when the hominid brain was still enlarging and reorganizing.

> No one can take from us the joy of the first becoming aware of something, the so-called discovery. But if we also demand the honor, it can be utterly spoiled for us, for we are usually not the first. What does discovery mean, and who can say that he had discovered this or that?
>
> GOETHE

FROM SHAMAN TO SCIENTIFIC REVOLUTION WAS A long haul too (thinking about that was my rationalization for my frequent rest stops). Just as there are some business-as-usual stretches of the New Tanner Trail, there are also some steep sections that slow you down.

And I didn't even have to find a path through these cliffs, only follow in the snowy footprints of the others up ahead. The first Indian to climb these cliffs had a much harder job than Alan, who was in the lead. When there's no trail, you use your knowledge of other trails—perhaps remembering that switchbacks are a good way to handle a steep gradient, rather than going straight up.

Yet what happens if you have *never* climbed a similar cliff before, don't have an instructor? And you don't know about switchbacking? Or about testing a handhold to make sure it will hold your weight (but looking first to make sure that your hand isn't going to disturb a rattlesnake)? Or about planning a tentative route or two, when you're still far enough back from the cliff to have a good view, rather than up close with a limited perspective?

Protoscience, without a body of tested methods to draw on, must have found it difficult going too. Many an explorer of the eclipse methods must have given up in disgust, rather like the naive hiker retreats after the first section of a cliff, feeling totally frustrated by the dead ends and all the back-tracking, worried about those shaking legs that had to hold too much weight for too long.

Modern science has a wonderful collection of methods and metaphors that often carry over from one field to another. I'm not thinking so much of the way my psychiatrist friends can gain insights into neurosis from the default settings of computer software (and how inappropriate settings cause machine equivalents of tunnel vision, premature closure, and other strange behaviors). Or the insight psychiatrists can gain from the strengths and limitations of the peacemaking techniques that primates are observed to use during times of social upheaval—that sort of animal model is pretty direct analogy, at least in comparison to the more abstract analogies and metaphors that sometimes develop. Some of the ways of thinking that oceanographers have developed to model the abrupt climate changes in Europe have certainly influenced my thinking about sudden mood changes in mental illness, those unfortunate patients whose violent behavior just seems to explode rather than gradually develop as anger builds. And the hardware and software problems of computers have given the new generation of neurologists some fresh ways of thinking about various other kinds of brain disorders.

Protoscience and modern science differ in some profound ways. As the biologist Mahlon B. Hoagland noted, modern science "is the natural searching within ourselves and our surrounds for explanations. It is the process of making comprehensible, by discovering and explaining with simple laws, that which had been a dark—and often frightening—mystery." But protoscience may well have been in the business of *creating* mystery instead, keeping secrets rather than explaining to others. In some fields, there is a post-modern reversion going on: For lack of sufficient public funding, basic biological research is becoming privatized in the biotechnology companies. New knowledge is closely held, rather than released in the public interest and widely discussed, as has been the academic tradition for basic research.

ABRUPT CLIMATE CHANGE REMINDS ME OF WHY RIT-ual was probably so important for protoscience, back before writing. Within just a few years (certainly less than a decade in some instances), ancient peoples must have gotten into big trouble because of the rains failing. Population levels surely crashed. Knowledge held only by a few people would have been lost because they all died before training a successor. The survivors may no longer have known that those solstice sightlines were handy for forecasting eclipses. They might merely have known that religious ritual required them to watch the sun and moon.

And that might have been enough to enable someone to rediscover eclipse prediction. The ritual itself might contain most of the building blocks needed for forecasting. The new Sun Priest might reformulate the rules a little differently than the dead ones, and so shift from one of the warning methods to another in the process. But the priestly power conferred by successful eclipse warning might reinvest the priesthood with a wide influence over whole tribes, even permit them to frighten off enemies with tales of their powers over the sun and moon. Without reading and writing, ritual and storytell-ing are what carry along the more abstract aspects of the culture.

THE TOP OF A MOUNTAIN IS CHARACTERIZED BY A curious restriction: As you approach it, your choices for where to step next become more and more constrained. You stop when you reach the top, because you can't go any farther. You can see farther as you approach the top, attain new perspectives—but the paths to those places first require a lot of backtracking.

Climbing out of the Grand Canyon is such a fitting metaphor for the ascent of science. As you reach the end of the path up the steep cliffs, you can indeed see farther—but the narrow path also starts to widen out onto a plateau. It's an accessible land of opportunity, with lots of new choices for your next step.

> It is a mark of modern ignorance to think that we have become progressively smarter. . . . Who is to say whether the task of tackling a problem without the benefit of a well-developed body of methods and information may not have required far greater intellectual vigor and originality than is needed [today] for proceeding from problem to problem within the safely established disciplines? Prehistoric, early historic, as well as medieval science have faced such a task.
>
> the historian THOMAS GOLDSTEIN, 1980

Notes

I should start by apologizing to all Southern Hemisphere readers for my descriptions of sun and moon directions that assume a Northern Hemisphere viewpoint. Readers in the tropics, even of the Northern Hemisphere, will also know that my descriptions of the sun's path through the sky will fail the test of generality in certain seasons. Most non-Northern-Temperate-Zone readers can, I suspect, make the relevant translations more reliably than the author, leading to my decision to leave these problems as "exercises for the reader."

I would like to thank Robert Euler, Donald Keller, Dabney Ford, and Astrida Blukis Onat for anthropological advice; Blanche Graubard, Leslie Meredith, and Katherine Graubard for editorial suggestions; Laurance Doyle, John DuBois, and Woody Sullivan for suggestions on the archaeoastronomy; Larry Stevens for a preliminary photographic survey of Cardenas, and the members of the Cardenas Solstice Expedition (Jack Bunn, John and Jim DuBois, Alan Fisk-Williams, Katherine Graubard, Karen Kepler, Lynn Langley) for their extensive help. The underground architect Malcolm Wells is responsible for converting my descriptions into valuable illustrations.

Chapter 1 CHRISTOPHER COLUMBUS, MASTER MAGICIAN

page
4 Brian Brewer, *Eclipse*, second edition. (Earth View, Seattle, 1991), p. 21. Partially reprinted in F. Richard Stephenson, "Computer Dating," *Natural History* 96(1):24–29 (January 1987).
5 The 29 February 1504 full moon was partially eclipsed for 103 minutes, totally eclipsed for 48 minutes, then took 103 minutes to uncover. At the midpoint of the eclipse, it stood over latitude 4°N, longitude 7°W. From J. Meeus and H. Mücke, *Canon of Lunar Eclipses −2002 to +2526* (Astronomisches Bro, Vienna, 1979). This implies that the eclipse began shortly before sunset/moonrise in Jamaica.
10 For some background on "after this, therefore because of this," see

the *Aplysia* chapter in my book, *The Throwing Madonna* (Bantam, 1991).

10 Elman R. Service, *The Hunters* (Prentice-Hall, 1966).

Chapter 2 HOW DOES STONEHENGE WORK?

17 Aubrey Burl, *The Stonehenge People* (Dent, 1987), p. 4.

20 Hunter-gatherers supernaturalistic: Service, p. 65.

23 Hacataeus, as quoted by the Sicilian historian Diodorus about 44 B.C.

24 R. J. C. Atkinson, "Decoder misled?" *Nature* 210:1302 (1966).

24 Gerald S. Hawkins and John B. White, *Stonehenge Decoded* (Dell, 1965).

25 Gerald Hawkins, "Stonehenge Decoded," *Nature* 200:306-308 (1963); Fred Hoyle, *On Stonehenge* (Freeman, 1977); H. C. Hostetter, in *Archaeoastronomy* 4:29-30 (1981); C. A. Newham, *The Astronomical Significance of Stonehenge* (John Blackburn, 1972); for a review, see Douglas C. Heggie, *Megalithic Science: Ancient Mathematics and Astronomy in North-west Europe* (Thames and Hudson, 1981), pp. 101-104. Hoyle has an excellent appendix on the geometry. Hawkins' use of the 56 holes is actually a warning scheme rather than a countdown; his eclipse seasons identify the same every-six-moons tendency for eclipses as my modulo-6 counting, and the 56 holes are used to count off the movement of the critical positions of full moonrise along the horizon.

26 Anthony F. Aveni, *Skywatchers of Ancient Mexico*. University of Texas Press. Harvey M. Bricker and Victoria R. Bricker, "Classic Maya prediction of solar eclipses," *Current Anthropology* 24(1):1-24 (February 1983).

28 Dating the Christmas supernova: Nigel Henbest, "New stars for old," *New Scientist*, p. 764 (18–25 December 1980).

32 Readers exposed to the New Math will recognize "Clinched Fist" as a *modulo-6* scheme; digital computers tend to use *modulo-8* "octal" and *modulo-16* "hexadecimal" schemes for internal computation, before translating the result to decimal.

34 Alison Jolly, "The evolution of purpose." In *Machiavellian Intelligence,* edited by Richard W. Byrne and Andrew Whiten (Clarendon Press, 1988), pp. 363-378.

Chapter 3 PICTURING THE ECLIPSED SUN WITH A HOLY LEAF

38 I also saw a near-miss near sunset: a solar eclipse didn't occur but one could see the shadow of the moon in the atmosphere, starting at

the horizon and expanding slightly before reaching the zenith. This cone shadow was visible for nearly a half-hour on the U.S. East Coast at the new moon in early February 1989; a partial solar eclipse occurred one month later, visible on the West Coast at midday.

41 The Pueblo peoples use crystals in kivas to reflect light entering through the smoke hole entry: A. M. Stephen, *Hopi Journal of Alexander M. Stephen*, edited by E. C. Parsons, *Columbia University Contributions to Anthropology* 23:959-962 (1936).

45 The Delicate Arch "spotlight" is present for a month before and after the summer solstice, whenever the sun's azimuth exceeds $293.5°$ but the sun is above $3.0°$ elevation; on first appearance, the spotlight is quite high and on Delicate Arch's stocky pillar to the north of the speaker's platform. Nearer the solstice, it starts below the pillar and angles up toward the speaker's platform. At the solstice, it starts well below the pillar (by about as much as the arch's height).

49 Robert C. Euler, George J. Gumerman, Thor N. V. Karlstrom, Jeffrey S. Dean, and Richard H. Hevly, "The Colorado plateau: Cultural dynamics and paleoenvironment." *Science* 205:1089-1101 (14 September 1979). And Jeffrey S. Dean, Robert C. Euler, George J. Gumerman, Fred Plog, Richard H. Hevly, and Thor N. V. Karlstrom, "Human behavior, demography, and paleoenvironment on the Colorado Plateau," *American Antiquity* 50:537-554 (1985).

51 Ray A. Williamson, *Living the Sky: The Cosmos of the American Indian* (Houghton Mifflin, 1984).

51 The Chaco Canyon "Sun Dagger" story is summarized by Anna Sofaer, Rolf M. Sinclair, and L.E. Doggett, "Lunar markings on Fajada Butte, Chaco Canyon, New Mexico," in *Archaeoastronomy in the New World*, edited by A.F. Aveni (Cambridge University Press, 1982), pp. 169-181; the sun-only part of the story may be found in A. Sofaer, V. Zinser, and R.M. Sinclair, "A unique solar marking construct," *Science* 206:283-291 (1979). See Williamson (1984) for a commentary and contrast to another Anasazi "Sun Dagger" at Hovenweep. Some doubts about the Sofaer et al. interpretation are expressed by Michael Zeilik, *Science* 228:1311-1313 (1985) and Jonathan E. Reyman, *Science* 229:817 (1985).

51 J. C. Brandt, S. P. Maran, R. Williamson, R. S. Harrington, C. Cochran, M. Kennedy, W. J. Kennedy, and V. D. Chamberlain. "Possible rock art records of the Crab nebula supernova in the western United States." In: *Archaeoastronomy in Pre-Columbian America*, edited by A. F. Aveni (University of Texas Press, 1975), pp. 45-58. Carl Sagan's *Cosmos* has a photograph of the Chaco Canyon pictograph on p. 232. The first report, from the area east of the

Grand Canyon, was William C. Miller, "Two possible astronomical pictographs found in northern Arizona," *Plateau* (Museum of Northern Arizona) 27(4):6-13 (1955).

51 Anasazi as astronomers: See John A. Eddy, "Archaeoastronomy in North America: Cliffs, mounds, and medicine wheels," chapter 4 of *In Search of Ancient Astronomies*, edited by E. C. Krupp (Doubleday, 1978); and Williamson (1984). Other rock shelters and Anasazi art, see the Preston's discoveries in *Arizona Highways*, pp. 22-25 (February 1983).

Chapter 4 TOP-DOWN AND BOTTOM-UP VIEWS FROM THE GRAND CANYON

53 Pamela Hansford Johnson, *The Unspeakable Skipton* (Scribner's, 1981).

56 D. W. Schwartz, R. C. Chapman, and J. Kepp, *Archaeology of the Grand Canyon: Walhalla Plateau* (School of American Research Press, Santa Fe, 1980-81).

56 Monsoon season, see Arthur M. Phillips III, "And then came the rains: Wildflowers in response to climate." *Plateau* 58(3):3-7 (1987).

61 Point of measurement of shadow would be when the sun's center is aligned with the celestial horizon; knowing about parallax and the atmospheric bending of light (which amounts to more than a sun/moon diameter near the horizon), a modern observer might want to use the point at which the sun's lower edge is a half-diameter above the horizon. By the time that the sun sits on the horizon, it has already set by a true horizontal.

62 The astronomer Gerald Hawkins noted the "moonrise not long before sunset" rule while awaiting a lunar eclipse at Stonehenge (see *Stonehenge Decoded*, p. 146) and suggests that one might predict the hour of the eclipse from the decreasing interval between moonrise and sunset on the nights preceding the full moon rise. My "more than a few diameters" rule requires some explanation. For the 6 August 1990 lunar eclipse, the moon's upper limb was at 1.8° when the sun's lower limb was on the western horizon; the eclipse started eight hours later, shortly before moonset. In the winter, when the full moon can be above the horizon twice as long as in summer, a greater range would be needed than four diameters. But "more than 3-4 diameters" should suffice to rule out lunar eclipses that might happen before midnight, and the occasional surprises would only be seen by the dedicated observers that stayed up all night watching.

63 The straight-line rule won't work for eclipses that are due to happen in the hours before dawn; the moon moves enough in its orbit during the night to shift the angles about eight moon diameters. For example, the evening of the lunar eclipse of 6 August 1990, which was seen in Seattle only in the hours just before sunrise, the moon rose across the celestial horizon at an azimuth of *119.2°* and seven minutes later, the sun set across the opposite celestial horizon at *295.6°* (so that the center of its shadow cone was at *115.6°*, about 3.6° north of where the moon rose). But simultaneous measurements, as in the shining streaks and shadows, would have had a separation of 4.9° for most of the time between moonrise and sunset. On most occasions when ten diameter separations occur, eclipses don't happen.

63 When an eclipse is due, the moonrise will often occur when the moon is in the penumbra, already getting less sunlight and with much of what it gets filtered through the earth's atmosphere. Thus the moon may appear redder than usual.

66 Observer's criterion: for example, when the rising moon is symmetrically positioned behind the sun priest, the setting sun should come to be symmetrically positioned behind the moon priest. Either upper limb or lower limb on the horizon will work, as long as the two observers have the same rule; note that the judgments are not made simultaneously but moonrise first, then sunset when it occurs.

If the horizons are truly flat (i.e., the celestial horizon, perpendicular to the vertical), equal rules for both observers are needed. But if the eastern horizon is elevated a little, the moonrise will occur slightly southeast of the true position; similarly an elevated western horizon also shifts the sunset angle to the southwest, creating a dogleg rather than a straight line between moonrise and sunset. One way to correct for a half-degree elevation difference (that's the approximate diameter of the sun and the moon) is to use the first glimpse of the moon (the "upper limb") but the sun when its bottom ("lower limb") is sitting on the horizon.

Two observers can evolve a correction for a larger elevation difference (given a standard observation site, say a high mesa) by introducing some lateral asymmetry. For example, the moon priest positions himself so that the rising moon's north side is touching the south side of the sun priest, as if framed in an L. The sun priest then watches to see if the setting sun touching the south side of the moon priest to form another L. If they stand far apart from one another, this sun-moon angle will be just short of 180°; if they move closer, the angle will shift down to 175°, etc. Thus a tradition might evolve of standing at a certain distance apart, just to create a correction angle that works locally for predicting eclipses. It's not something that you might stumble into, for discovering the straight-line method initially, but a tribe that moved from its original locality to the plains or mesas might discover that some slight changes in their original symmetrical method would still function correctly. Unless the horizon elevation is uniform (as I postulate for bank-and-ditch at the megalithic monuments), the correction would vary with the seasonal change in the direction of the sunset.

66 E. C. Parsons, *Pueblo Indian Religion* (University of Chicago Press, 1939), pp. 86, 181.

66 Florence H. Ellis, in *Archaeoastronomy in Pre-Columbian America*, edited by Anthony F. Aveni (University of Texas Press, 1975), pp. 82-83.

67 I first mentioned (though rather cryptically; it was a note added in page proof) some eclipse methods in *The River that Flows Uphill: A Journey from the Big Bang to the Big Brain* (Macmillan, 1986), p. 113.

71 Horizon calendars: See Williamson (1984) and Stephen C. Mc-Cluskey, "Historical archaeoastronomy: The Hopi example," in *Archaeoastronomy in the New World*, edited by A.F. Aveni (Cambridge University Press, 1982), pp. 31-57.

Chapter 5 THE VIEW FROM AN ANASAZI CAVE

75 Jacob Bronowski, *The Origins of Knowledge and Imagination* (Yale University Press, 1967 lecture, published in 1978), p. 9.

77 One of the great misnomers in naming apes is due to the preoccupation with cavemen. The common chimpanzee's Latin name is *Pan troglodytes*. The common chimp and the bonobo ("pygmy" chimpanzee, *Pan paniscus*) are certainly the most versatile of the extant apes "but have *never* been observed to live in a cave, except at a zoo. Sleeping nests in trees are more their style. There are also some birds with species name *troglodytes,* but they really do live in holes or caves.

78 Typical topics of cave art: the anthropologist Dale Guthrie, in a talk at University of Washington (17 February 1988).

86 Pocket transit measurements are not considered adequate evidence by themselves; magnetic anomalies due to iron in the sandstone are always a possibility, and hand-held instruments are not as accurate as those mounted on a stable surveyor's platform. The best evidence is a picture of sunrise or sunset in the inferred location; if one cannot return at the winter solstice (and Anasazi Valley's steep approaches can be dangerously icy in the winter), a surveyor's instrument (a

theodolite) can be used to measure the angles, and a sun sight can be taken (calculations are easily done to determine its azimuth and elevation at any time of day) to use as a reference direction for the measurements of the corners. Unfortunately, you can't see the sun from many of the sites in the summer, because of those shadowing overhangs. At the more open sites such as Chaco, I did take sun sights to correct for local magnetic anomalies, rotating the pocket transit atop a level table (a plastic plate atop a camera tripod) from the sun's direction (known from calculations based on latitude, longitude, and time) to the sightline, using the magnetic bearing differences to infer its azimuth. In the light of the subsequent successes with solstice alignments from kivas, the uncorrected measurements from the pocket transit at Anasazi Valley may well be reasonably close.

91 The roof of Perfect Kiva is not entirely original; it had to be repaired by the archaeologists. And probably strengthened against foolish visitors. Many decades ago, a large horseback party of tourists came down Anasazi Valley "and all 40 of them had their group photograph taken while standing atop Perfect Kiva. The thousand-year-old roof cracked."

92 Perfect Kiva sunrise and sunset views: While winter solstice photographs are the best way to settle the uncertainties of pocket transit measurements, one must also remember that the tilt of the earth's axis has decreased somewhat in the last thousand years, about 0.1° (one-fifth of the sun's diameter). The estimates are close enough so that they can "be made to fit," the usual expedient being making an assumption about what the Anasazi used as their point of measurement. Upper limb "first gleam"? Or lower limb visible? Or nicely nestled into a corner? I develop the latter idea subsequently, at Chaco Canyon, but the sun is so high in the sky (15°) by the time that it rises behind the staircase that framing the exposed sun on its bottom and left side won't work at Perfect Kiva. An obscuring frame must be used, and the horizon feature at *135°* seems perfectly suited to the purpose.

93 Examples of posts or pillars as foreground sights for pivoting about: The Stonehenge heel stone is perhaps the best-known foreground sight, though daily movements about a standard sight are seldom mentioned in the megalithic literature. For the Anasazi, see the analysis of pivoting by Michael Zeilik and Richard Elston, "Wijiji at Chacho Canyon: A Winter Solstice Sunrise and Sunset Station," in *Archaeoastronomy* 6:66–73 (1983), briefly summarized by Ray A. Williamson, *Living the Sky: The Cosmos of the American Indian*

(Houghton Mifflin, 1984). Proposals for levered sunset sightlines to the offshore islands of neolithic Scotland explicitly include the notion of daily sidesteps: A. Thom and A. S. Thom, in *In Search of Ancient Astronomies*, edited by E. C. Krupp (Doubleday, 1977), pp. 55–65.

Chapter 6 SIGHTLINES TO SOMEWHERE

95 Elman R. Service, *The Hunters.* (Prentice-Hall, 1966), p. 68. "Too many kivas": There was a time when any round subterranean room was called a kiva, but it is now clear that 1) some kivas were rectangular and above-ground (such as the one at Turkey Pen Ruin), and 2) some round foundations are not kivas in the Pueblo sense of a ceremonial room and clubhouse. Kivas tend to have a ventilation shaft down their south wall, drawing air down to a fire pit beneath the ladder through the roof opening; there is usually a deflector plate in the floor at the end of the air shaft, so that the flames are not blown sideways into the room. Round rooms without such features are more likely to have been storage rooms, etc.

107 One has to do this probability analysis for each site, and the analysis in the text is predicated on a situation such as Stonehenge, with panoramic views. At Betatakin, for example, there are only 2–3 nice features in the west that could be used. But there isn't a 60° spread on both east and west horizons from which to choose, as the alcove faces south and severely constrains the view of both southeast and southwest horizons from anywhere in the alcove, so the one chance in 120 is more like one in 25. The text also doesn't mention moonrise and moonset extremes, which tend to expand those 60° sectors by another 8° on each end, at least at the latitude of the Four Corners sites.

108 Driving north from Phoenix along the freeway, one comes upon a particularly striking mesa. The road signs indicate that it is named Table Mesa. I always imagine the many Mexican–Americans living in Arizona as having a good laugh as they drive by; whoever named it seems not to have known that he was repeating himself.

110 Velma Garcia-Mason, "Acoma Pueblo," in *Handbook of North American Indians*, volume 9, edited by Alfonso Ortiz (Smithsonian, 1979), pp. 450–466.

110 Quote from Ward A. Minge, *Acoma: Pueblo in the Sky* (University of New Mexico Press, 1976).

114 Paul R. Ehrlich, *The Machinery of Nature* (Simon and Schuster, 1986), p. 234.

114 The Hopi-Navajo contrast suggests looking at the two populations

for twinning rates and other data that might indicate some evolutionary specialization along the r-K spectrum that I discussed in *The Ascent of Mind: Ice Age Climates and the Evolution of Intelligence* (Bantam, 1990), Chapters 6 and 7.

115 Some Native American tribes reconciled the lunar and solar calendars by adding (as the Jewish calendar does today) a thirteenth lunar month every three years. The best evidence is Alexander Marshack's "A lunar-solar year calendar stick from North America," *American Antiquity* 51(1):27-51 (1985).

116 Ruth F. Benedict, *Zuni Mythology*, vol. 2, pp.66-67 (AMS Press, New York, 1969).

117 R. W. Effland, Jr., A. T. Jones, and R. C. Euler, *The Archaeology of Powell Plateau: Regional Interaction at Grand Canyon* (Grand Canyon Natural History Association, monograph 3, 1981).

118 The Hopi history is from Stephen C. McCluskey, "Historical archaeoastronomy: The Hopi example," in *Archaeoastronomy in the New World*, edited by A. F. Aveni (Cambridge University Press, 1982), pp. 31-57.

120 Crow Wing (1925), cited by McCluskey (1982), p. 38.

Chapter 7 CORNERING THE SUN IN A CANYON

126 Chris Kincaid, editor, *Chaco Roads Project, Phase I: A Reappraisal of Prehistoric Roads in the San Juan Basin* (U.S. Department of the Interior, Bureau of Land Management, Albuquerque, 1983). I thank the Chaco archaeologist Dabney Ford for her interest and advice.

131 Robert H. Lister and Florence C. Lister, *Chaco Canyon: Archaeology and Archaeologists* (University of New Mexico Press, 1981), Figure 80.

133 I saw a possibility for accurately measuring summer solstice at the North Rim of the Grand Canyon: at summer solstice, the rising sun on the far-distant horizon is framed by a cliff a few miles to the northeast of Cape Royal, at least if you stand in the right place. The horizon is quite low, allowing *Open Frame* (as well as *Obscuring Frame*). The distance means that the day-to-day sidestepping is considerable, even near the standstill. There used to be a ruin in the vicinity of the summer solstice turnaround, but all is now a parking lot for Angel's Window.

135 The equinox yes-or-no is all part of a general principle of measurement, applicable to anything that varies back and forth: measure it when it is rapidly changing, not when it has slowed down to reverse direction. For example, to determine noontime when the sun is

highest in the sky, don't sit there measuring the length of a shorten-
ing shadow and waiting for it to begin lengthening. Instead note the
time when the sun is partway up in midmorning, and then note the
time in the afternoon when the sun is back down to the same
elevation angle and thus casting a shadow of the same length as in the
morning. Halfway between the two times was noon, when the sun
was highest in the sky. It's probably what the Hopi are doing when
they second-guess the Sun Priest: they watch the sun pass a characteristic horizon feature weeks before the solstice, and again weeks
after the solstice, and so they know that halfway in between was the
exact day of the solstice. And, hopefully, their Soyal celebration was
indeed held that day.

134 The great kiva's perfect north-south alignment is reviewed by Ray
A. Williamson, "Casa Rinconada, a twelfth century Anasazi kiva,"
in *Archaeoastronomy in the New World*, edited by A. F. Aveni (Cambridge University Press, 1982), pp. 205-219.

Despite the north-south symmetry, the four large pillars that
supported the great kiva's roof (which no longer exists) are in the
solstice sunrise and sunset directions, at least when the sun is about
15-16° high in the sky (see Williamson's Table 1). I would note that,
were there a center smokehole in the roof in the manner of Hadrian's
Pantheon, an oblique sunspot would cross a pillar several hours after
dawn; one imagines a band around Post D in the northwest, above
which the sunspot never reached, the maximum height being
reached on the winter solstice sunrise (and similarly for sunset on
Post A in the northeast). In the days before the summer solstice, the
sunspot would descend Post C in the southwest, reversing when
reaching a band at the same height. And similarly for sunset on
Post B.

135 The sun cornered, touching an edge plus the horizon at bottom, is a
very different criterion than first gleam (sun's upper limb, as tabulated in almanacs). Since the sun rises along a line tilted about 40° to
the horizon at winter solstice, this also means that the first gleam is
in the corner. The main problem with using that first gleam as the
criterion is that, unlike the case of a flat horizon, you don't know
what part of the sun's rim you're seeing "until the sun rises a little
farther and more of the circle can be seen." The main problem with
so framing the sun is that you have to look at the entire sun, which
can be rather bright. And so such framing only works near the
horizontal, when the sun's brightness is filtered by the extra-long
path through the atmosphere. At higher elevations, it would never
work.

Chapter 8 HALF A VIEW PROVIDES THE CLUE

139 Member of Taos Pueblo, quoted by Jeannette Henry, Vine Deloria, Jr., M. Scott Momaday, Bea Medicine, and Alfonzo Ortiz, editors, *Indian Voices: The First Convocation of American Indian Scholars* (The Indian Historical Press, San Francisco, 1970), p. 35.

148 The necklace beads would also make a good ruler, a route into counting.

149 The equal-angles rule works exactly only at the celestial horizon, since the sun rises at a shallower angle to the horizon in the southeast than the northeast; at a 5° uniform horizon elevation, the maximal error is 1° (two sun/moon diameters along the horizon). But the overnight changes are often much larger than this, and so tend to be the limiting factor in determining "how close" is close.

158 The observer's path also needs to be horizontal; if it goes uphill and down, it will destroy the virtues of the bank's elevated-but-level horizon. I'd recommend digging a shallow ditch along the observer's path, filling it with water and a little chalk. And then after the water evaporates or drains, fill the ditch with rocks, up to the height of the high water line. You also need a standard-height observer (sighting along the mark on a staff) or each observer having his own solstice markers.

153 Actually, what you want is symmetry of the observer's path around the sightline to equinox sunrise, and that isn't really due east because of the elevated horizon. So in looking for leveled observer paths (and this applies as well to the north-south room walls discussed later), one might hope to see a few degrees offset from a perpendicular to due east. Not compensating would, however, cause so little error that the failure to find such offsets means nothing.

154 The slit-shadow method is also inaccurate because it uses a shadow line rather than direct viewing of the sun/moon. Shadow lines are fuzzy, especially if the window is far away; move your eye into the shadow and you'll start to see the edge of the sun; continue moving and the rest of the sun will uncover. That penumbra, due to the half-degree diameter of the sun, is why any serious comparison of arcs is going to be hard. While longer levers would nominally improve things, they will also spread out the penumbra more. So looking directly at the sun/moon, and positioning it in a frame, is far more accurate. If you don't have room to put your head in the path, reflecting the light via a crystal seems a likely substitute.

154 Lack of evidence for sun-watching from kivas: M. Zeilik, in *Archaeoastronomy* 7:76–81 (1984).

Chapter 9 WHEN SUNRISE IS AN ILLUMINATED EYE:
WINTER SOLSTICE SEEN FROM THE BOTTOM
OF THE GRAND CANYON

159 Arlette Frigout, "Hopi ceremonial organization," in *Handbook of North American Indians*, volume 9, edited by Alfonso Ortiz (Smithsonian, 1979), pp. 574.

163 Split-twig figurines: R. C. Euler and A. P. Olsen, *Science* 148:368–369 (1965).

164 Mischa Titiev, "Old Orabi: A Study of the Hopi Indians of Third Mesa," in *Papers of the Peabody Museum of American Archaeology and Ethnology* (Harvard University), 22(1) (1944).

164 The Hopi month names are discussed by S. C. McCluskey (1982), pp. 44–46.

166 Since perihelion is currently in January and the earth travels faster in its elliptical orbit then, the two half-years (from solstice to solstice) are an unequal number of days, but this potential error will make little difference in warning of lunar eclipses in the several hours after sunset.

166 Only horizon positions associated with the "sun's ruler" are relevant; when full moon rises outside the sunrise extremes, eclipses are impossible.

168 Alexander M. Stephen, 1893 letter to J. Walter Fewkes quoted by McCluskey (1982).

169 D. W. Schwartz, R. C. Chapman, and J. Kepp, *Archaeology of the Grand Canyon: Unkar Delta* (School of American Research Press, Santa Fe, 1980–81).

169 Prayer shrines may be well away from habitations: McCluskey (1982), p. 34.

175 Pack rats: Donald F. Hoffmeister, *Mammals of the Grand Canyon* (University of Illinois Press, 1971), pp. 137–139.

183 A reading error of about 0.5 meters would still make the Cardenas levered sightline quite a scientific measuring instrument: that's about 20 arcsec of declination. And without metal, just an *objet trouvé*.

184 The ancient axial tilts (obliquities) are calculated from the Fourier series given by Andre Berger in *Nature* 269:44–45 (1977). With a declination decrease of 0.83° (corresponding to 1.38° along the horizon at 36° latitude) since the maximum tilt 9,500 years ago, and allowing for the ruin being 7.4 meters below the ridgeline viewing position, the 3,100-meter distance to the window yields a turn-around position of 84.5 meters toward the ruin from the present site

82.3 meters from its nearest corner. This also includes minor corrections for the observers being 0.3 meters shorter (based on Mesa Verde Anasazi) than myself and for the 1982 solstice occurring 12 hours after the observations were made. The 82.3 meters measured along the contours of the hiking path overestimates the straight-line horizonal distance by about 3.0 meters, suggesting that the ancient turnaround was 5.2 meters inside the ruin, whose diagonal is 9.2 meters.

185 Wear and tear at Cardenas hilltop ruin: Besides weather, there is that from contemporary visitors; not only is there a major hiking path passing the ruin, but boatloads of river-runners camp just below, every night during the summer. For someplace not accessible by automobile, this ruin has a lot of visitors annually—one reason why the archaeology ought to be done soon.

185 R. H. Lister and F. C. Lister, *Those Who Came Before* (University of Arizona Press, 1983), p. 16.

185 The turnaround of all turnarounds: The Cardenas hilltop ruin's site might merely have been the first such turnaround that was observed, 9,000-10,000 years ago (and even this date is subject to what part of the ruin corresponds to turnaround—the south edge, the center, etc.). To say that they *knew* it was the turnaround of all turnarounds is a considerably greater claim, one that I am not making; that would have required them to be around a few thousand years earlier, watched their winter turnaround viewpoints marching further and further northeast, and then seen them reverse drifting, leaving a structure at the extreme location.

Chapter 10 THE LONG ASCENT: FROM SHAMAN TO SCIENTIST

187 James Clerk Maxwell, quoted in *The Sciences* (July 1986), p. 9.

194 Richard W. Wrangham and Jane Goodall, "Chimpanzee use of medicinal leaves," in *Understanding Chimpanzees*, edited by Paul G. Heltne and Linda A. Marquardt (Harvard University Press, 1989), pp. 22-37.

195 "Respect" via novel act: Jane Goodall, *The Chimpanzees of Gombe* (Harvard University Press, 1986).

195 Female chimpanzee hierarchies: Frans de Waal, *Chimpanzee Politics: Power and Sex Among the Apes* (Harper and Row, 1982). See also Goodall (1986) and Toshisada Nishida, "Social interactions between resident and immigrant female chimpanzees," in *Understanding Chimpanzees* (1989), pp. 68-89. And for the ape language debate, see

Sue Savage-Rumbaugh, "Language acquisition in a nonhuman species: Implications for the innateness debate," *Developmental Psychobiology* 23:599–620 (1990).

200 Mahlon B. Hoagland, *The Roots of Life* (Houghton Mifflin, 1977), p. viii.

200 Frans de Waal, *Peacemaking Among Primates* (Harvard University Press, 1989).

202 Thomas Goldstein, *Dawn of Modern Science* (Houghton Mifflin, 1980).

Index

ABOUT THE AUTHOR

WILLIAM HOWARD CALVIN was born in 1939. He studied physics at Northwestern University and then spent a year at the Massachusetts Institute of Technology and Harvard Medical School, making the transition from physics to biophysics. He then moved to Seattle, where he studied the primate visual system and cellular neurophysiology, receiving a Ph.D. in physiology and biophysics in 1966 from the University of Washington. Following his doctorate, he remained at the University of Washington; he has been associated with the Department of Neurological Surgery, Department of Physiology and Biophysics, Biology Program, Department of Zoology, and the Honors Program of the College of Arts and Sciences. More recently he has become an affiliate professor in the Department of Psychiatry and Behavioral Sciences. Most of his research concerns the brain circuitry for planning novel movements, such as nonroutine speech, "what if" scenarios, and ethical choices. He has written on human biological evolution in *The Throwing Madonna: Essays on the Brain; The River that Flows Uphill: A Journey from the Big Bang to the Big Brain; The Cerebral Symphony: Seashore Reflections on the Structure of Consciousness;* and *The Ascent of Mind: Ice Age Climates and the Evolution of Intelligence.*